# DESIGNING
# *Wine Cellars*
## PLANNING / BUILDING / STORING

## Dagmar Kreutzer and Martin Palz

4880 Lower Valley Road, Atglen PA 19310

**Cover Design:** DSR / Werbeagentur Rypka GmbH, 8020 Graz, Austria

**Photo Credits:** Cover picture: Foto Nutz, Waldhofen/Ybbs Pictures in text were kindly made available by the authors.

The contents of this book were checked by the authors and publishers to the best of their ability, but cannot be guaranteed. Legal liability is ruled out.

*Schiffer Books are available at special discounts for bulk purchases for sales promotions or premiums. Special editions, including personalized covers, corporate imprints, and excerpts can be created in large quantities for special needs. For more information contact the publisher:*

Schiffer Publishing Ltd.
4880 Lower Valley Road
Atglen, PA 19310
Phone: (610) 593-1777; Fax: (610) 593-2002
E-mail: Info@schifferbooks.com

For the largest selection of fine reference books on this and related subjects, please visit our web site at

**www.schifferbooks.com**

We are always looking for people to write books on new and related subjects. If you have an idea for a book please contact us at the above address.

This book may be purchased from the publisher. Include $5.00 for shipping. Please try your bookstore first. You may write for a free catalog.

In Europe, Schiffer books are distributed by
Bushwood Books
6 Marksbury Ave.
Kew Gardens
Surrey TW9 4JF England
Phone: 44 (0) 20 8392 8585; Fax: 44 (0) 20 8392 9876
E-mail: info@bushwoodbooks.co.uk
Website: www.bushwoodbooks.co.uk

Copyright © 2010 by Schiffer Publishing
Library of Congress Control Number: 2010932666

Translated by Dr. Edward Force
Designed by Stephanie Daugherty
Type set in Florens LP/Exotc350 Bd BT/Futura Hv BT/Zurich BT

ISBN: 978-0-7643-3637-9
Printed in China

# Contents

# *Introduction*

## WHY STORE WINE?

In the development of wine, storing it is the most important side issue in the world—it begins with the vintner and ends in the glass. Essential changes in the wine take place precisely because wine is stored under specific conditions with certain prerequisites. Thus it is to be regarded as a living thing that is subjected to very certain changes in every phase of its development. Beginning in its youthful phase, the wine develops over the course of time, in order to enter a more or less long period of maturation, which is better ended by its consumption than its aging. Thus there are many principles and also possibilities for wine storage. The most important perspective for us consumers is to drink wine when it tastes best!

Aside from the different requirements that the wine producers on the one hand and the consumers on the other place on wine storage, they do have one thing in common: Both must span the time from the bottling of the wine to its sale or enjoyment so that nothing in the wine's quality is lost. Though the vintner primarily stores wine in large containers (wooden barrels, steel tanks), the consumer is concerned with the storage of wine in bottles. But there are also wines that are aged already bottled by the vintner in order to attain a certain bottled maturity.

In the following chapters, all the prerequisites and principles that are of importance in storing wine will be examined—from the characteristics of a wine through the storage requirements to the construction requirements that exist for wine storage, and the possibilities that you may already find in your cellar.

First, though, just a few general ideas as to why wine should be stored.

*Storing Wine — Why?*
*Collecting Strategies*

*Storing Wine means being able to enjoy the right wine at the right time!*

Traditional (top) and modern (bottom) wine storage.

One must actually begin with the purchase. Whoever buys a little wine will soon notice that, what with the application of varying technologies and philosophies, there is a broad spectrum of wine styles. The difference for some years now is not merely between red and white wine, but beyond that to reductive-maintained young wines, classic and especially strong types of wine, powerful stored wine, oxide-free white wines (sherry), sweet wines, plus fruity young red and full-content red wines. But these are just a few examples of various wine types that require individual storage conditions.

---

Fresh, fruity wines reach their optimal drinking maturity in the first two years after bottling; strong storage wines and red wines have potential for a storage of definitely more than three years.

---

To the extent that the wine producer has not yet achieved a certain readiness for bottling, the consumer can decide how long the wine—presumably under optimal conditions—should mature in the bottle. To be able to work properly for this bottle-maturity, it is advisable when buying wine to purchase several bottles of the same wine. This is true above all for wines with storage potential that are not going to be drunk on every occasion.

The vintner knows
the right point in time
when the wine is ready
to be bottled—
bottle-maturing occurs
at the vineyard as well as
in the private cellar—
while the drinking
maturity of the wine is
up to the consumer!

Also, please do not forget to buy a supply of wine that you wound open a bottle of at any time without doubts.

When you purchase large quantities of wine, then in transporting it, the car trunk is its first storage place. Make sure that the wine is not exposed to high temperature variations, especially in summer, since this influences the quality of the wine considerably. After a long transport trip, the wine needs to rest. The constant moving and shaking of the bottle influences both aroma and taste. Two to three weeks' time should be allowed after the bottling or transport of the wine, so that it can become calm.

*The way of the wine to the individual wine cellar is—unavoidable: careful transportation.*

*Visually impressive wine storage with exclusive space available.*

Along with the necessary bottle maturing and the obtaining of a wine supply, speculative reasons for wine storage also exist in many cases. Wines that steadily gain quality and goodness with increasing maturity are also more expensive as a rule. Above all, French red wines from renowned chateaux obtain the highest prices at wine auctions. It is exactly these wines that contradict what was said above, for these wines are usually not drunk!

## Collecting Strategies

Wine is one of the few living foods that can get better with advancing age. It is a means of nourishment as well as enjoyment, which goes through a certain development and thus always reveals itself from a new side. This process is called the maturing or aging process, in which constituent parts of the wine change through contact with oxygen. Tannin, coloring, and aromatic materials—primary as well as secondary aromas—are changed in their content and replaced through new connections of ingredients with new characteristics—the so-called tertiary aromas. As already noted, a certain supply of wine is needed to experience such a development.

In acquiring a supply of wine, one should consider that some wines need a longer storage time and other wines attain their full drinking flavor in a few years. These qualities are usually indicated by the price charged for a bottle of the wine, but

*Getting information directly from the vintner is always rewarding, especially in social wine drinking.*

not exclusively! While strong white wines (storage wines) and heavy red wines only attain an optimal harmony through their bottle maturing, for reductive, fruit-emphasized wines, a shorter bottle storage time is surely an advantage. The basis of any collecting strategy, though, should be to enjoy the wine when it has reached its drinking high point. In addition, it is often the vintners themselves who gather wines from many lands in order to compare or even measure them with their own wines in sensorially exciting tastings.

If you collect wines for comparison tasting, always do it according to a concrete theme—kind of grape, soil, region, year—for otherwise you will soon lose the overview and simultaneously cause more confusion than you create clarity!

The face of the wine is the vintner and the label—both strengthen the likelihood of remembrance!

Always store several bottles of the same wine; it will afford you new impressions at every opening.

# Storage Ability of Wine

Among foods, wine probably belongs to the types of products that can be stored. Yet, in terms of the extent of wine's storage ability, there are great differences depending on the preparation of the wine based on the combination of its ingredients, and surely also upon the type of storage. For that reason, even specialists are not able to say exactly in advance how long a wine can be preserved. Many wines maintain their qualitative high point over many years. While others quickly deteriorate after their zenith of pleasure and lose their freshness and typical qualities.

## The Ripening of Wine —
## Why Old Wine?

For the old-fashioned concept of aging and in the language of wine, the word "maturation" is often used. In both cases it refers to the changing

*The main thing: store them lying down!*

*Fully ripe grapes are a prerequisite for long storage ability—and not only for Sauvignon blanc*

of wine through storage over a certain period of time. Wine, as long as it is not drunk right after bottling, changes in terms of its appearance and aroma. This is attributable to the oxygen that forms new wine ingredients through its great need to combine, as well as enzymes, which can also cause an oxidation reaction through specific replacement processes. The two have in common that these reactions occur according to both temperature and light. Thus special attention should be devoted to special storage!

Wines develop differently according to maturity, vintage year, and type of preparation. As long as this development occurs positively, it is called maturation, but if the wine loses quality or was too weak, one speaks of aging. Exactly between maturation and aging there occurs the high point of enjoyment, at which the wine has attained its optimal maturation for drinking.

**To be able to trace the development of a wine, it is necessary to have several bottles of that wine on hand. In this way one can trace the development of its bottle maturation very well and get to know the same wine in varying stages.**

## Factors in Aging Wine

For the storage ability of wine, not only the enzymes and oxygen molecules already named on the "destroyer side" are responsible. To a considerably greater extent, the actual components of the wine, such as alcohol, acids, extra ingredients, and in particular the components of the grapes, the skin, pulp, and seeds, play their roles. Together they create a complex structure, which in turn should lead to individual, unmistakable wines. Again and again, though, wines that are anything but unique and unmistakable appear on the market—wines that are produced and bottled in unimaginably great quantities under homogeneous conditions.

The uniqueness of wine derives on the one hand from its origin, which does not allow comparable wines to be produced on other soils, localities or expositions, and on the other, from the individuality of the vintner, who applies his own experience and conception of quality in turning grapes into wine. Both the origin and the vintner are equally responsible for what amounts of what ingredients are contained in wine.

*Classic stone terraces in the Wachau provide support, as well as soaking up warmth.*

*A high plain in Eppan, South Tyrol, has a special climate because of the surrounding mountains.*

*The gentle slope of a hill in Glanz, southern Styria.*

# Alcohols

Ethyl alcohol (ethanol) is the main product of alcoholic fermentation, its amount depending on the sugar content of the grapes and the degree of fermentation. It makes up between 9 and 13% of the volume (equaling 72 to 104 g/l), brings extract and full flavor, and is, in its quality of carrying aroma, also the heart of a good product.

Methyl alcohol (methanol) should occur in wine only in very small amounts (17-230 mg/l). Even if one or another mythological product is said to have had an overly high methanol content, the actual amount depends on the intensity of the mash contact. Higher alcohols (fusel oils) are also found only in meager amounts (150-700 mg/l), but because of their nature are important aroma or taste carriers. Glycerin as a primary byproduct of alcoholic fermentation occurs at about 5-10 g/l and has a positive effect on the fullness and harmony of a wine.

# Polyphenols

## Coloring Agents (Flavonoids, Anthocyane)

In grapes, the color is imbedded in the berry skin. Through suitably long standing time of the mash (fermentation of the crushed berries), a more or less high content of coloring materials is leached out, along with tannins. Red wine contains red and

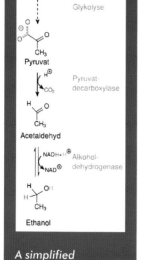

Glukose

Glykolyse

$O$
$CH_3$
Pyruvat

Pyruvat-
decarboxylase
$H^⊕$
$CO_2$

$H$ $O$
$CH_3$
Acetaldehyd

$NADH+H^⊕$ Alkohol-
$NAD^⊕$ dehydrogenase

$H$ $OH$
$H$
$CH_3$
Ethanol

*A simplified portrayal of alcoholic fermentation—from grape juice to wine*

blue vegetable coloring matter, called oenin, which belong to the group of anthocyanes. In 100 grams the content is about 30-750 mg, of which only 30-50% (10-300 mg) gets into the wine through the working of the grapes. Anthocyanes are sensitive to light and temperature, so during storage it must be assured that constant low temperatures and darkness prevail. Through maturing and aging, a color change takes place, affected by oxidation, from highly colored via orange to brown. Anthocyanes also have a health-promoting, so-called antioxidative effect, which can occur in much greater amounts than those of Vitamin C and Vitamin E. In the human body, anthocyanes bind free radicals and thus slow cell oxidation. This decreases fat storage (plaques) in the blood vessels and cuts down arteriosclerosis and thus serious heart and circulatory illnesses.

*Fully ripe blue grapes…*

*…make a strong, very dark red wine!*

*Young, reductively*　　　　*Ripened*　　　　*Highly colored, oxidized*

**Tannins (Phenols)**

Also known as tannic acid, these are organic substances that create a tart, slightly bitter taste. They are also essentially responsible for how long a wine is storage-capable. Since tannins come from the grape skins, stems, and seeds, processing is decisive for the extent of phenol content. White wines contain some 200-300 mg/l, red wines up to 1000 mg/l of phenol in all. A higher phenol content has a positive effect on the durability and storage capability of the wine to the extent that the complex structure of polyphenols is much harder to destroy with oxygen than in light wines.

# Smell and Taste Substances (Aroma)

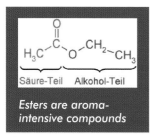

Säure-Teil    Alkohol-Teil

*Esters are aroma-intensive compounds*

*L-ascorbic acid (Vitamin C)*

Smell, bouquet, fragrance, and taste materials in wine are mainly transitory organic combinations that are present only in very small amounts. Differing according to the type, many components (primary aromas) arise in the assimilation or maturation, and join with other materials in the later development: Fruit esters (carbonic acid—alcohol), aldehyde, fusel oil compounds (higher alcohols), and others.

Some 800 different substances in wine that originally occur both in the skin and the pulp of the grapes have been differentiated. The so-called terpenes, which are originally bound to sugar, are released only in the process of fermenting and thus become aroma-effective (secondary aroma). During storage, though, they change, through the influence of oxygen and enzyme effect, into so-called tertiary aromas. The total content of aroma materials contained in wine still does not amount to more than 0.8-1.2 g/l, and about half of it consists of fusel oils (see Alcohol chapter).

## Vitamins

In wine one finds a series of vitamins that are important to life, plus mineral materials and trace elements that are absolutely necessary for metabolism. The most important vitamins that occur in wine come from the Vitamin B and C groups and affect the nervous system positively, influence glandular functioning and muscular tension, and intervene to regulate the sugar content of the blood. Vitamin C may be added to wine in the form of L-(+) ascorbic acid (E 300) as a means of anti-oxidation. Such wines, to be sure, develop a very positive freshness in the first months after bottling, but with longer storage they change to a negative effect. Thus the ascorbic acid becomes a cause of UTA (untypical aging tone).

Do not try to acquire your minimum daily requirement for vitamins in the form of wine!

## Acids

In the end, a whole series of acids help to determine the taste of a wine. Wine acids and apple acids are the quantitatively determining acids by which in "mature years" a definite "overhang" of wine acid occurs. In very ripe grapes one also finds more citric acid than in under ripe ones. When the wine goes through a biological degeneration of acids, apple acid turns to milk acid at a 2:1 ratio, giving the wine a mild, full flavor. The content of carbonic acid also lets one know whether the wine is a reductive young one or one of greater age. A high content of apple acid has a rather negative effect, since apple acid changes considerably more strongly in the process of storage than do milk and wine acids. The apple acid also gives the microorganisms optimal nourishment conditions, which in turn leads to unstable wines.

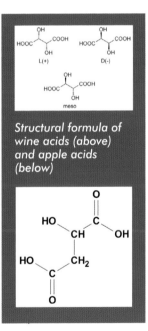

*Structural formula of wine acids (above) and apple acids (below)*

## Carbohydrates (Sugar)

The main sugar elements in fruit juice are grape sugar (glucose) and fruit sugar (fructose), which are changed in this order by the yeast to ethanol, $CO_2$, and warmth (alcoholic fermentation). The degree of the fermentation determines the content of the reducing sugar in the wine (remaining sugar). A remaining quantity of sugar can also come from the Arabinose—a naturally occurring, unfermentable simple sugar.

---

**The remaining sugar content in grams per liter, like the alcohol content and the specified volumes, is part of the required information on a label, and is, in Italy among other lands, also stated in percentage of the volume (%vol.) and designated as potential alcohol.**

---

Wines that, on the basis of an interruption in fermentation, show a heightened amount of remaining sugars (over 15 g/l) are especially in danger of carrying out a "post-fermentation." On the basis of their sugar content they are, to be sure, very storage-capable, but should be checked from time to time.

## WATER

The daily WATER CONSUMPTION of 2 TO 3 LITERS should be drunk in addition to wine, not in the form of wine!

80-85% of the proportional volume of wine consists of water, which creates life-engendering prerequisites for the plant. Water is a solvent and transporter of nutriments, comparable with the function of human metabolism

## EXTRACT SUBSTANCES

Extract materials are non-evanescent components whose content depends on many factors. The main components are glycerine, sugar, permanent acids, mineral materials, albumen, tannins, metals, and many others. To be sure, there is no legal minimum extra content anymore, but the wine should clearly show over 20 g/l of sugar-free extract (total extract minus remaining sugar).

## Metals

The trace elements iron, potassium, calcium, natrium, magnesium, manganese, copper, zinc, and others occur in wine in amounts that are so favorable that they fulfill a valuable nutritional function and can be seen from as invaluable from a health standpoint.

## Mineral Substances (Ashes)

Originating from the grape skins, the content of mineral materials (ashes) in wine varies very much (2-3 g/l). Most of them are salts of already noted acids: tartaric (wine acid), phosphate (phosphoric acid), malate (apple acid), and others. The main component among the acids in wine, with 650-950 mg/l, is potassium. Through the wine-stone detritus (potassium hydrogen tartrate), the higher content, around 1,000 mg, is considerably decreased.

## Sulfite Content

The sulfur content in wine has an important influence on its durability. The salts and esters of the sulfuric acids ($H_2SO_3$), also called sulfite, do not, of course, belong to the original components of wine, but are formed from the deliberate addition of sulfur oxide (SO2) in the process of vinification, so as to bring about a certain reductivity, and durability. The characteristic of the added sulfur is aimed at the release of oxygen (O2) and the prevention of microbial and enzymatic activity. The oxidization thus prevented—similar to the browning of an apple after it is bitten—leads to a considerably longer-lasting freshness and liveliness of a wine.

*Required labeling according to EU allergy guidelines for all foods that contain allergic materials.*

A wine without sulfite content is possible, to be sure, but not worth striving for.

## Sealing Systems

The storage ability of wine is influenced considerably by the use of certain bottle closings. The time is

*Natural corks—long a symbol of value*

*Agglomerates (pressed cork) —the less costly variants, also in qualitative terms*

*1-, 2- sliced cork—the attempt to improve*

*Plastic corks—color as optical attraction*

long past when only crown corks, natural corks, and products made from cork dominated the situation. At the moment we find ourselves in a sort of breakaway mood. Natural cork, agglomerate cork (pressed cork), sliced cork, plastic stoppers, screw tops, and glass stoppers are the systems that one finds today. Each of them finds justified use in various realms. The vintner must decide what optical appearance he wants, and above all, what prerequisites the wine to be bottled possesses. The consumer, on the other hand, is interested only in how the stopper affects the storage duration and the type of storage. Stoppers let more or less oxygen pass through, so that the wine matures and, after the sulfuric acid is released, oxidizes to either sherry or vinegar, or if remaining sweetening agents are present, brings about post-fermentation.

Natural corks afford a familiar picture of maturing, but also the danger of tasting the cork (2, 4, 6 trichloranisol) (TCA)) and unsealed bottles—"leakers." Good natural corks guarantee a very long preservation, but should still be replaced or recorked after 25 to 30 years at the time of refilling and resulfuring. The life span of a natural cork, which can measure from 38 mm to over 60 mm, plays only a minor role in the preservation of wine. Very often, corks over 48 mm are not used, and if they are, it is mainly for visual reasons and as a symbol of the value of a wine—but the durability is not extended!

Pressed or agglomerate corks, and also sliced corks, are only partially suited for closing bottles and so are used only for certain qualities. They consist of the leftovers from natural cork production plus adhesive or binding materials, and thus are suited only to very short storage. Sliced corks are made with two to four slices, on the basis of natural corks.

Plastic stoppers are best suited for short storage, since they possess the great advantage over natural corks of having a neutral effect on taste while looking just as good. They are made in almost every color and size, and thus can be part of the bottling process. Plastic becomes brittle in time, though, and does so independently of whether the stopper contacts the wine or not, which leads to a somewhat unusual maturing. The taste of red wines with plastic stoppers is clearly better after many years than similar white wines.

Crown corks, now as before, are found mostly in liter and piccolo (0.2 l) bottles. Because of the good storage qualities, unlike the high occurrence of rust, crown corks made of rust-free stainless steel are frequently used with, for instance, pearl wines.

While the storage and maturing qualities with glass stoppers cannot yet be tested thoroughly, it is rather assumed that they come close to the screw cap, and they are being used more and more. Introduced by ALCOA in 1924, the gas-tight MCA 28 (28 mm x 15.5 mm) has also been used for wine since the 1970s.

The great breakthrough in the realm of quality wine also succeeded, to be sure, in using the Stelcup 30 x 60 (30 x 60 mm), but its appearance and storage qualities leave something to be desired. The part that is decisive in tight sealing is a layered seal sheet that is pressed through the screw cap. This leaf is a disc covered with Saran (polyvinyl chloride), aluminum or tin, which at first lies loose in the cap and is best suited for long storage thanks to the pressure of putting on the cap. Wines closed with screw caps are usually very reductive when opened, and thus need more time after opening to develop their taste properly.

*MCA 28, Stelcup, Vonolok — caps introduced over the years*

# Principle of Origin

To the question of how long wines of a certain origin can be kept, it can be affirmed that in general the storage ability of wine depends less on the origin of the wine than on the type of preparation. In the realm of wine, there is the principle of origin, according to which all wines are to be labeled according to the precise geographical region, or at least the country, of origin, in which the grapevines grow and the grapes ripen. In Austria, there is even a differentiation for white as well as red wines between classical winemaking and Lage or Ried wines.

*Classic wine production
from several sources*

*Selective development
of individual vineyard
locations (Riede)*

According to law, there must be a declaration of the classical winemaking on the rear label or outside of the sight area, in which the relevant data of the classical process are declared. Among the white wines there are mostly dry wines that have a distinctly fruity taste, are very reductive and have been exposed to no further vinification influences, such as Barrique storage or biological acid breakdown. Among red wines, it can occur that a BSA in combination with Barrique storage has taken place, of which only very little or none at all can be sensed. The grapes for these wines can come from various vineyards within one community, large area or winemaking district.

Ried or Lage wines, on the other hand, were made from grapes grown in one very definite vineyard in one clearly defined area (Riede, Lage) under special influences (sun rays, altitude) and special circumstances (soil). The special feature of these wines is the uniqueness and rarity in which they were produced. Often Lage wines are stored in small (Barriques) or large (600 l and up) wooden barrels to lengthen the durability of the wine through the tangible influence of the oak wood (tannin), but also to give the wine more complexity. The biological breakdown of acids that provides additional fullness through the reduction of apple acid to milk acid is found most commonly in white wines of the Burgundy types, but in general in red wines.

*Classic 225-liter or
300-liter Barrique
barrels, usually made
of French oak*

*The renaissance of the large wooden barrel, good acid penetration with moderate storage*

## Terroir — Region

The "Terroir" concept, coming from the French, doubtlessly ranks among the most overused words in the wine vocabulary. It describes the impression of the wine on the basis of its origin and the inter-play there among (micro-) climate, geology (soil), topography (terrain), and soil composition. Night and day temperatures, precipitation distribution, sunshine hours, slope, and soil porosity are fac-tors that, along with the influence of the cultural technique, determine the character of a wine. Thus "terroir" is something that can be defined neither exactly in numbers nor in sensory impressions, but is rather a collective concept that stands for the typicality and assignment of a wine to a definite ori-gin. "Terroir wines" rank among the most strongly expressive and durable of all wines.

*Mighty shell chalk soil at the Zieregg in Styria forms the characteristic of the wine!*

# The Right Wine for the Right Occasion

It is practical, not only from the vintner's point of view, to always have several different wines in the cellar, both classical and Lage wines, red wine, rose/ and white wine. One should thus make sure that the classical wines reach their high point fairly

NOTE PARTICULARLY
WHEN buyING WINE
THAT classic wINE should
NOT be OPENED TOO late
ANd LAGE wINE
NOT TOO SOON!

quickly and taste best in their younger years. Lage wines, on the other hand, need—as long as the vintner has not already carried out part of the bottle maturing in his own cellar—several years before they have reached their drinking high point, whereby one can definitely keep it so that it is less of a tragedy to open a wine before its high point of enjoyment than after!

Which wine is to be kept on hand naturally also depends on whether the wine is to be used as an aperitif, with a meal, or as a main attraction. With the help of a good varied wine cellar, the suitable wine is always on hand for the right occasion, and above all for the right mood.

## SHOppING FOR WINE

Like the enjoyment, the buying of wine is an event accompanied by emotions. When you have made the decision in favor of a certain style of wine, there are a hundred wines from the most varied localities and countries. Then too, wine buying is not done only from the vintner or Vinothek anymore, but more frequently from the specialty shops and grocery stores. Thus an emotional tie, namely the relationship with the vintner, disappears, and the conditions of production (labeling, capping) takes on a greater role.

*Vintner supplied wine shop*

# WHEN IS THE RIGHT TIME TO BUY WINE?

In an investigation of the wine-buying process in markets and grocery stores, the Institute for Commercial Sciences of the Commercial University of Vienna has ascertained that the decision to buy is very short-term and spontaneous. Nearly half of the asked people needed a maximum of two minutes to buy the wine of their choice. Aside from the choice, buying wine is usually done very shortly before drinking it, which means that the wine is chosen for the occasion and thus should stand on the shelf ready to drink. That is a very convenient but at the same time expensive way of buying wine. Even though it involves little capital investment and storage capacity, it is the choice made mainly in simple gastronomy.

Does one really think about what pleasure one misses when one unnecessarily eliminates buying wine directly from the vintner? Meeting the people who care for natural beauty and health affords the wine consumer with a feeling of authenticity.

When one buys directly from the vintner, one naturally also has the chance to learn something of the origin and character of the wine. Such "special attunement" often leads to friendly connections between the producer and consumer, so that many a person has sought out "his vintner."

Sprouting of grapevines in the spring (April)

Grape blossoms in summer (June)

Foggy atmosphere in autumn (October)

**Time of rest in winter (January)**

# Storage Conditions

Temperature

Humidity

Cleanliness and
Strange Smells

Light

Storage Angle

Transport and Shaking

Order and Accessibility

*In particular,
wine that will be
raised up longer
needs the right
storage conditions.*

Wine is one of the few living means of nour-ishment and pleasure that needs a maturing and storage process for its development. Wines also age differently under different conditions.

If you consider several factors, you can increase your enjoyment of wine considerably. Properly stored wines last longer and mature better.

Many of the strict cellar rules, though, still come from earlier times. Most wines, because of present-day progress in the vineyard and cellars, are much less sensitive to influences from their environment than they were twenty years ago. Much may take place somewhat more loosely today. Thus success-ful storage and maturation of wine is less complex than many a wine lover might think at first.

## TEMPERATURE

Of all climatic factors, the air temperature is especially important for storage. At lower tem-peratures, the biological and chemical reactions run more slowly, the maturing process is slowed down, and the formation of mold on bottles and walls is limited. In an ideal case, the wine stor-age place should maintain a constant low room temperature between 8 and 12 degrees Celsius, 8 to 10 for white and 10 to 12 for red wines. A storage temperature of 15 degrees C should not be exceeded, since at temperatures of 20 degrees C and above thermo-labile components (such as albumin) disintegrate and can lead to disturbance. Too-low temperatures (below 5 degrees C) lead im-mediately in unstable wines and with long storage of all wines to separation of crystals (winestone and others)—so-called "depot building." It is decisive, though, that the cellar temperature during the entire storage time stay as constant as possible, and above all that no greater changes than 4 de-grees C during the year. Cellars that show great temperature variations—in winter clearly under 10 degrees, but in summer over 20 degrees C—are always critical for the maturing process and quality maintenance of wines over a long time. Temperature variations, in fact, influence the development of fresh supplies negatively.

The wine also copes with slow deviations from ideal temperature values over a long period better than with major temperature changes.

**When a cellar warms slowly from 12° C in winter to 20° C in summer, not much happens to the wine. Problems occur when the temperature changes strongly every day or every week.**

*Constant low storage temperatures slow the development of wine*

The wine spreads out in the bottle and pulls itself back together, the cork suffers, and finally the wine begins to "cry" around the cork, leaving behind a sticky deposit around the cap. Besides, it ages so fast that it never reaches its qualitative high point. White wines in particular lose their desired freshness.

**The principle is: Low temperatures delay a ripening of the wine in the bottle. Higher temperatures, on the other hand, hasten the maturing process through more vigorous activation of the microorganisms in the wine.**

Before you set up a cellar, you should take measurements with a thermometer at various places and make notes of them. Certain corners will be warmer or cooler than others. Eliminate or decrease the causes of these temperature variations. For example, wrap hot water pipes with insulating materials and avoid cold drafts. Seal walls, ceilings and doors to heated parts of the house with simple insulation plates. These methods will keep the cellar some 2 to 4 degrees cooler.

A further possibility would be to install a cooling system.

---

**During the hot months, be sure to ventilate! Utilize cool night air and try to keep warm outside air out of the cellar by day. Keep doors and windows closed as much as possible!**

---

Temperature changes caused by outside air, even when displaced in time, can make themselves known even in deeper cellars.

Shrubbery often used to stand before the entrances to wine cellars as weather buffers. The wine hedge with its leafy roof provided cooler temperatures.

Note: When the temperature in the storage room changes, the relative humidity also changes. This can lead to the formation of condensation!

# Humidity

You can raise the humidity of the air by covering the floor with a layer of gravel and watering it, or by setting out flat pans of water.

In an ideal case, the relative humidity amounts to more than 50%. If the humidity of the air is too low, corks can dry out and become loose. Thus the entrance of air and oxygen becomes possible. The wine oxidizes, discolors to a golden brown, takes on the familiar sherry or old-wine shade, and finally "breaks." Vinegar bacteria also can penetrate into the wine past a dried-out cork and likewise make it unusable.

A much greater problem is humidity that is too high. This leads to spore formation or even to an unwanted mold formation on the cork. This fungus can grow through the cork in time and will then give the wine the feared cork taste. Such a wine

*Cork mold caused by humidity that was too-high*

is no longer drinkable. There is also the danger of the labels coming loose. The latter can happen with a humidity of over 35%. When storing in the original carton, one should also remember that the stability of the cartons when they are stacked is very much weakened by high humidity, softening and bending the lower cartons, which then tend to tip. Cartons of various sizes and shapes, in particular, show very high instability when stacked. Above all, the danger of tipping is especially great when cartons come from the vintner's or dealer's cool storehouse and are transported at high temperatures—which is unavoidable in summer. Condensation occurs on the glass walls of the bottles, which can not only loosen and destroy the labels, but also can lead to mold formation and to softening of the carton. In general, wines should only be stored in cartons temporarily, as they afford neither the view nor the rest that the wine needs, since restacking will be frequent. In addition, cartons possess their full stability only when they are completely filled with bottles.

Overly high humidity can be removed with a dehumidifier. But it is costly—in terms of both its purchase and operation. For small cellar spaces, such means as water removal, better air circulation, and sealing of moisture sources, such as very damp walls, often suffice. Measurement with a hygrometer provides clear information!

Fasten labels at the right time with a rubber band.

Only temporary storage in the original cartons!

Check the humidity with a hydrometer

...only intended as temporary storage...

# Cleanliness and Strange Smells

Do not set up
a wine cellar close to
a garage, furnace room,
laundry or vegetable
storeroom.

Before you store wine in your cellar, you should clean the cellar as thoroughly as possible. It is best to use an odor-free disinfectant, in order to kill mold, insects, and other organisms. For old cellars it is recommended to paint the walls with whitewash.

Wine breathes and thereby takes on intense smells. Strange smells, such as heating oil, motor oil, gasoline, detergents, paint, vegetables or decay create a problem for the storage of bottled wine. These intense smells can result in the wine taking on an atypical smell and taste over the years through the porosity of the cork, or even render the wine unpalatable. Fungi and other organisms can also be transmitted by other foods.

Good and sufficient air circulation is, therefore, important for any wine cellar. Circulation prevents moldy smells and decay. Mold can in fact form because of insufficient air movement.

*When air circulation is not strong enough, mold forms despite sanitizing.*

*Maximum cleanliness in a historic vaulted cellar.*

# Light

As charming and practical as it may be to place wine bottles decoratively on display in the dining room or kitchen, one will do better to store them in darkness. Darkness treats the wine better. Problem areas are, above all, windows, light shafts, and ventilators. White and sparkling wines in light bottles are especially sensitive. The direct sunlight warms the wine and allows it to age faster. The wine loses in quality. Naturally, one needs artificial light to use the cellar. But it should not be too bright, and should never be turned on for longer than is necessary.

Wine loves light only when it comes into the glass!

Wine bottles, depending on the color of their glass, let different amounts of UV light through. Very dark bottles, especially brown ones, provide the greatest UV protection.

Make absolutely sure that no UV light gets into the cellar.

For very old and sensitive wines, one should also consider covering them (for example, with an old blanket).

Brown bottle— best UV protection

Green bottle— good optics, medium UV protection

White bottle— no UV protection

But choose your wine according to its taste and not just for the color of the bottle that most tempts you to buy it.

*Practical and effective use of indirect lighting.*

*A definite recommendation of standing storage*

# Storage Angle

Whether one stores wine lying or standing depends first of all on the closure system. Yet it is quite possible that it is even stated on the label how the wine is best stored. Here is what one sees on a bottle of Vinho Verde DOC from northern Portugal. Wines that were sealed with a natural cork should always be stored lying down. The cork must be touched by the wine so that it can preserve its elasticity and seal the mouth of the bottle well. A harmful invasion of oxygen is thus prevented, and only oxidation with the available oxygen allows the wine to mature as is desired and necessary.

Bottles with a crown cork, screw cap or glass stopper can also be stored standing up. A reason not to use such stoppers is that the lack of air change, often necessary for wine maturation, is not possible to the extent desired. A fact favoring using these stoppers, though, is that the freshness and youthfulness of a wine are maintained longer.

Some collectors arrange their cabinets so that the bottles are inclined very gently backward. Thus, deposits form on the bottoms of the bottles, and the corks are still moistened. The labels should point upward, so that they are easily legible and the deposit settles on the back of the bottle.

# Transport and Shaking

Before you can store your wine systematically in your own wine cellar, you must first transport it. It is essential—especially for wine-buying trips in the summer, in which you purchase large quantities of wine—that the temperature of the wine should never rise too high.

**When you come home with your purchased wine, you should absolutely let your wines lie quiet in the cellar for a few days before you consume them.**

Through bouncing and shaking during transport, the wine disintegrates and must regain its inner stability. That applies less to the younger, fruity wines. Old, ripe wines with deposits in particular lose their quality temporarily.

Constant vibration from road traffic, subway trains running under the house, railroad traffic, heavy machinery, and vibrations from household machines prevent wine from coming to rest, so that it can never be enjoyed in its best form. Racks protect the bottles a little.

# Order and Accessibility

It is not good for wine if one often picks it up, moves it around, and replaces it while looking for a different bottle in the cellar.

As soon as wine is stored, it should be able to rest. So avoid moving wine to get to other bottles. Every wine should be easy to find. Use labels and/ or a cellar book.

## Organization and Cellar Book

Every owner of stored wine should make efforts to keep order among his wine bottles. An easy-to-see, systematic storage system is very much to be recommended. Either one divides his wine storage according to wine qualities, types, and vintages, or according to the origin of the wine, by lands and growing regions.

*Neat—but hard to find anything without labels*

**When possible, the natural warmth of a wine cellar should be used by storing the red wines in the upper part and the white and rose wines in the lower area.**

Also important for a clearly seen storage division is a sensible system of labeling shelves and bottles. The exact designation of the storage place is thus so important, because one can then find every single

Possible means of recognition include adhesive labels, wash-off tags, and numbering bottles bottle quickly and surely without having to search through the entire contents of the cellar every time.

Whoever wants the best for his wines can also mark the bottle bottoms with adhesive tags. When wines are stored in wooden cases, the side with the wine name and vintage should be visible.

Part of every well-organized wine cellar is a well-kept cellar book. Along with recording the most important dates of the wine—name, maker, vintage, the number of bottles, time of optimal maturity, purchase date, source, plus the sale price, recording the date and occasion for consumption are also of interest. Besides that, there should be enough space for any notes. With a cellar book in which one can list bought and consumed wines, the "circulation" in the cellar can be followed easily.

### Vinothek

*Wine-geographical information makes important data readily available*

The "Ideal software" firm offers, under the name of "Vinothek" (wine library), an electronic inventory system for industrial applications. The Vinothek is a specific organizational tool for wine. With it, all specific entries, from the region through the quality class to the certificate of origin, can be found and evaluated. In combination with the storage administration, a precise organization of all the bottles is possible. In addition, many wine regions already make maps available that can be used by the shopper. The attachment and presentation of labels and an evaluation by taste according to the international 20-point system complete this addition. The Vinothek is just as interesting for the wine trade as for the upper-class gastronomy or the private wine enthusiast. For epicures and wine fans, an attractive version of FAKTMANN, reduced for simpler wine administration, is available. Check with the company to ascertain if English language versions of these programs are available. A quick search of the Internet will also put English language programs with similar features at your fingertips.

The intuitive usefulness of "WinWein" (WinWine, a German abbreviation for Windows Wine Database) makes it a wine software that is also usable by "software-inexperienced wine fans" and eases their immersion into the interesting world of wine. The graphic service instructions make "sorting" and "updating" of your wine data simple via detailed register cards (dates of origin, storage and evaluation dates, notes, cellar book, and foods). An easy "mouse operation," plus the additional access to all program functions by "hot-keys," allows you, for example, to bring up the label of your favorite wine with just one click of the mouse. Similarly, you can let the diminution of your recorded wine supply per wine be shown. The basic data of the wines (name, type, country, vintage, producer, etc.) are so-called major entries for the data bank. Here the program requires, as its only necessary tool, just the name of the wine to be added. A clear understanding should also be oriented to the fields of the numerous ways of sorting and the ideal drinking maturities. Along with sufficient space for further notes on every wine, an Internet site that also contains further information on your wine can be listed and reached directly from there.

## WinWein

The intuitive usefulness of "WinWein" (WinWine, a German abbreviation for Windows Wine Database) makes it a wine software that is also usable by "software-inexperienced wine fans" and eases their immersion into the interesting world of wine. The graphic service instructions make "sorting" and "updating" of your wine data simple via detailed register cards (dates of origin, storage and evaluation dates, notes, cellar book, and foods). An easy "mouse operation," plus the additional access to all program functions by "hot-keys," allows you, for example, to bring up the label of your favorite wine with just one click of the mouse. Similarly, you can let the diminution of your recorded wine supply per wine be shown. The basic data of the wines (name, type, country, vintage, producer, etc.) are so-called major entries for the data bank. Here the program requires, as its only necessary tool, just the name of the wine to be added. A clear understanding should also be oriented to the fields of the numerous ways of sorting and the ideal drinking maturities. Along with sufficient space for further notes on every wine, an Internet site that also contains further information on your wine can be listed and reached directly from there.

With the possibility of adding labels, your wine also takes on a "face" immediately.

## Weinsave

The Swiss economic researcher and wine aficionado Roland Waefler has developed a very extensive program that reaches from the wine-cellar administration through an epicurean journal to data administration, which makes new entries easier and appropriate evaluations possible. This system allows you to gather pictures of various wines, no matter whether they involve labels, grape types, areas of origin, producers, or photos of gatherings at which you have enjoyed the wine. Besides the more than 100 photos and 700 maps that are included in the program itself, the most important photo formats like BMP, JPG, GIF, TIF, and PCX are supported. Additional functions allow vintage evaluations to be consulted and a wine lexicon to be referred to, wine to be ordered very simply or a wine for a meal to be recommended, which can be done according to your notes of your own personal taste.

A particularly practical application allows for the possibility of working with barcodes. With a suitable scanner, codes already present on bottles or labels can be read, and new codes can be added. Wines once registered (via barcode) can then be booked out, especially when a bottle is taken out of the stores. Combined with a mobile calculator (Handheld, Palm, Laptop…), this allows a very simple administration of the wine supplies on hand and their data, which can be actualized simply and with every opportunity in the wine cellar or at wine-tasting gatherings.

Through the use of a special scanner, barcodes can be read and thus time can be saved!

## Vinefine

The specialty of this software is its compatibility with the largest German wine portal, Wein-Plus.de. Thus, it is guaranteed that a large number of German and international wines, complete with relevant data and comments, can be loaded directly into your own administrative program. These, as well as your own entered data, can be sorted according to several criteria and also be put on paper in appropriate printing processes. The entry of new wine sources is eased to the extent that most wine-growing countries and regions, as well as types of grapes, are already included and only need to be selected. Besides appropriate

This vastly shortens the preparation time for an interesting wine tasting!

filter functions, there is also the possibility of portraying the drinking maturity of the wines graphically for better orientation, thus making this vital information much easier to see at a glance. Whoever would like to generate a tasting list from his or her own wine cellar can do this, with all wine-relevant data, in this up-to-date version of wine administration.

## VitisVinifera

This wine-cellar and taste administration data-bank program offers the user a detailed but clearly set-up layout. Interesting, especially for its very valuable wines, is the possibility of using the information about market prices, the development of which can be shown very clearly in a chart or table. The detailed evaluation—eye, nose, taste, potential—by a 20- or 100-point or a freely defined point system, plus the listing of optimal drinking maturity, are just as practical as already listed types of grapes, growing regions, storehouses, and classifications. The stated data can then be expressed in the form of lists according to self-defined criteria, as well as a data sheet on just one product.

DETAILED WINE EVALUATIONS, INCLUDING EVALUATIVE EXPERIENCES, CAN BE DOCUMENTED BY THE 20- OR 100-POINT SYSTEM.

## Wine XT

This wine software is intended for all Apple users. Developed for Macintosh, it is wine-cellar software plus taste administration. Clear portrayals and assured high use flexibility make working with this program simple and pleasant. The usability of the material in several languages, including Japanese, is noteworthy, as is the use of small symbols for better and quicker use. For faster entries and further use of data, as also in Winesave.ch, the use of barcodes and Vinoté tags is supported.

## Digital Cave

Many of the wine administration programs have similar functions. The actual wine storage (virtual cellar), which can be formed graphically and true-to-life on the PC, is definitely something new. At first the setup (windows, doors, walls, shelves, wine

THE OPTION OF BUILDING YOUR
OWN VIRTUAL WINE CELLAR
ALWAYS LETS YOU KEEP AN EYE
ON IT. BUT IT ONLY MAKES
SENSE WHEN YOU DOCUMENT
EVERY CHANGE!

cases) is understood, whereby several shelf forms are available, and later additions or adaptations can be made without problems. Then wines that are found in your data bank can be placed simply in the desired spot, moved, or taken out again. The program automatically delivers information about the available storehouse items or the value of your cellar. The movements that thus take place in your wine supplies are checked in lists and can be expressed for easier reading or exported as a package of data.

## WeinWare

This is a very extensive economic system that goes far beyond the needs of and requirements of a private wine cellar. Functions like the preparation of mailings, detailed evaluations concerning customers, suppliers, and articles are primarily helpful for wine dealers and agencies.

As with many software providers, demonstration versions as well as shareware are made available for testing purposes on the appropriate homepage. You should explore the possibilities to obtain the appropriate program suited to your needs. The fullness of the offerings leave scarcely anything to be wished for, and if anything is lacking, one or another company can be found who will definitely suit its program to your individual wishes. You can easily find others who offer software solutions via the Internet contacts in the addenda.

## The Traditional Wine-Cellar Book

While a number of software solutions can be had at present, the handwritten wine-cellar book still has something to offer in terms of style and tradition. No additional technical arrangements are necessary to keep it always up to date and ready, and the handwritten entries have a much higher emotional content.

You can form your own wine-cellar book very simply with a bound pad or a loose sortable system, or even turn to the bookselling trade for a prepared volume. A particularly original example has come to us from Dr. Olaf Mueller-Soppart; it was made out for a supply on hand in 1898.

# Physical Structure

## Damage from Dampness and Its Causes

Water is the most frequent cause of structural damage. Moisture damage occurs because of rain or ground water, when the water from outside penetrates into the building. Water in gaseous form generally goes the other way under normal conditions.

Dampness damage frequently occurs, especially—but not exclusively—in old buildings. The most frequent problem areas are damaged roof drainpipe mouths, paved yard surfaces, cellars of buildings, laterally pushing slope water, cracks in the façade, increasing dampness, and building dampness.

Causes of dampness damage are often found quickly. Roof drains and outflow pipes can sometimes develop holes, or their discharges are pointed directly at the cellar wall. A damp cellar wall, though, can also be caused by new yard pavement. With such additional pavement, rain and other surface water sources no longer soak slowly into the ground as before, but instead flow more quickly off the newly paved surface. In many cases, the surface tilts slightly—a tilt often not visible to the naked eye—in the direction of the cellar.

Large spots on the cellar walls usually indicate slope water coming from the side. If the building is out in the open, its foundation is exposed to draining precipitation. The wall then absorbs the dampness, according to its material and construction. Via the smallest hollow spaces, so-called capillaries, the moisture is then conducted on into the foundation.

Only sealing the wall from the outside and drainage that makes sure the water around the foundation can flow away as quickly as possible will help. Within limits, cement coatings, painting with tar, or plastic or tar foil are useful. These materials, of course, are not particularly ecological, but they do fit the form of old foundations better than rigid cement.

Let as little moisture as possible into the building!

*Rain and surface water should be directed away from the foundation*

If one wants to protect the cellar floor or walls from rising dampness, a horizontal isolation must be built into the foundation.

Historical structures are often equipped with air channels around the foundations, to drain off occurring dampness.

___

**Sealing from inside, for example with spackling plaster, usually just makes the wall look dry on the surface. The dampness rises farther up until it finds a surface from which it can evaporate. In the worst case, this occurs in the living area above.**

___

*Drainage: Catching and removing ground water*

*Outside isolation: A coat of tar with a foam covering*

Formerly the cellar floor remained unsealed. Thus moisture came in, but it was wanted so that fruits and vegetables could be stored well. High foundation walls were built to prevent moisture from reaching the ground floor. The cellar ceiling was thus above the ground level, as shown in the Archduke Johann House.

On the one hand, wall surfaces provided enough evaporation surface presence; on the other, cellars were constantly ventilated by high window openings. Later, horizontal seals were built into the outside walls. But at first, the cellar floor remained open and thus damp. Later on, the cellars were expanded. Watertight materials were used for walls and plaster, and tightly closing windows were installed. The evaporation no longer took place, and moisture damage increased.

*Use cellar windows for ventilation!*

But moisture in a building can also have another cause, namely structural dampness. Thus, after the building phase, there is always a high degree of moisture in a massive structure from the water used to prepare the building materials (such as concrete, mortar or plaster), which dry out only after some time. In bricks that takes about one year, in concrete up to three years.

# Mold and Its Formation

Mold fungi are primitive plants. They make meager demands on their environment. Since they cannot carry out photosynthesis, their food supply is limited to organic materials.

*Black cellar mold (Cladosporium cellarii) is neutral in smell and sight, but usually a problem.*

Mold fungi find good growing conditions in slightly sour environments (pH values between 4.5 and 6.5). They thrive at temperatures between 0-40° Celsius. Light and darkness have scarcely any effect on their growth, but water is a real growth factor. Usually a relative air humidity of 80-85% on the attacked material is sufficient to begin the growth of a mold fungus. If the mold is to be combated effectively and enduringly, no surface cosmetics with soda, chalk or vinegar is sufficient. Its living conditions must be destroyed!

Causes of mold formation are insufficient ventilation, cold bridges, and badly absorption-capable materials like concrete, stone, metal or glass.

*Mold formation on a wall is one of a cellar's greatest problems.*

**If mold has already formed in a cellar, it must first be removed (vinegar essence or soda solution). The affected places should then be painted with whitewash or mineral paint, because in such a climate the fungus grows badly.**

Mold formation can be avoided by climatic separation of the areas. The use of absorbent materials and sufficient sealing, drying of cellar air, and naturally ventilation prevent mold formation.

# CONdENSiNq MOisTURE

Dealing with dampness in the air in cellars often causes great problems. This can involve the fact that man has no sensory organ with which he can measure dampness in the air. Only extreme dryness or very high dampness will be noticed. But when one sees water vapor, then it is no longer a case of dampness in the air, but rather of condensed little drops of water.

*Mold fungi also partially destroy the surface they grow on, as here on bricks.*

At a certain temperature, air can take up only a very specific amount of moisture. This is called absolute air humidity.

In the rarest cases, air takes up so much moisture that it is fully satiated. The relative humidity gives the percentage of the maximum satiation dampness actually present. For example, 50% relative humidity means that the air contains half as much moisture as it could hold at that temperature. The amount of moisture that the air can hold depends on the temperature. It increases when temperatures rise and decreases with falling temperatures.

If warm, moist outdoor air gets into a cool cellar, it cools down. In the process, the relative humidity can climb to values near 100% according to the cellar temperature. If the air temperature, for example, sinks even further on cold wall surfaces, the humidity is no longer able to stay in the air as water vapor, but partially precipitates as condensed water. The temperature at which water vapor condenses is called the dew point.

*The only way to check the humidity is with a hair hygrometer.*

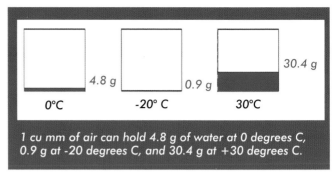

1 cu mm of air can hold 4.8 g of water at 0 degrees C,
0.9 g at -20 degrees C, and 30.4 g at +30 degrees C.

The condensation process always begins at the coldest place in the room. Usually it is a windowpane or a badly sealed wall surface.

In order to prevent the formation of condensation as much as possible, it is best to ventilate cellars only during the cool night hours in the warmer part of the year!

**Example:** The dew point at an air temperature of 22° C and 70% humidity is 16.3° C. A temperature difference of fewer than 6° C thus already causes a wet precipitate.

**Example:** If one closes the bathroom door and turns on the shower, window and mirror surfaces cloud up in a short time. If one then turns on the hair dryer, the air dries and can absorb more moisture. Windows and mirrors become clear again.

**Example:** Room volume 50.0 square meters, maximum moisture 860 grams at 20°C, the temperature in the room falls some 5°C, maximum amount of water 650 grams at 25° C; 210 grams precipitate as dew (*sketch*)!

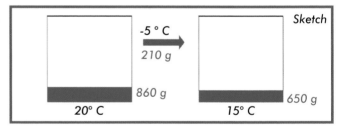

To avoid condensation water, there are thus two possibilities: Either one changes the temperature or the humidity of the air in the room. The humidity in a cellar is usually influenced more easily by ventilation.

**Attention:** Condensation is not only an optical blemish. If the water condenses on a surface, mold forms as a result. But if it condenses in the inside of a structural component, it can lead to soaking through and thus to the reduction of stability and insulation against heat. Rotting and damage by harmful organisms are also possible then.

# Water Vapor Diffusion

Only under ideal circumstances is the greatest part of the moisture transported out of the interior of a cellar through a change of air. About 2% of the moisture in the area goes into the open directly via structures. The passage of water vapor through structures is called diffusion. The structural, physical problem exists particularly because materials that do not let water through can be penetrated easily by water vapor. This water vapor diffusion does not damage the structure if the moisture really reaches the outside. Thus, the structure of the wall is of great importance. To be sure, structures do resist this diffusion somewhat (water vapor: Diffusion resistance $\mu$ [mu]; $\mu$ air $= 1.0$), but they can and should not prevent the diffusion entirely. Brick has a vapor-diffusion resistance of 8, chalk sandstone of 15, and concrete of 70.

The better insulating layers should be on the colder outer side, the more watertight layers inside, and the material open to diffusion outside, so that the moisture that has penetrated can be conducted away better. Therefore the outside of the wall should also not be coated with watertight paint. Watertight materials should be constructed so that they can absorb and discharge moisture without thereby influencing their functional ability.

---

**The diffusion resistance of the building materials should decrease from inside to outside! If this is not so, it will result in watertightness within the wall structure and thus to damage from dampness.**

---

Problems are caused by coldness bridges, the choice of the wrong materials, damaging moisture barriers or watertight paint outside.

The dew point of a structure should, when possible, be situated where the condensing water does no damage and can easily be directed to the outside.

# Absorption Behavior of Materials

Absorption describes the ability of building materials to absorb excess water vapor and give it off again when it needs to. This effect takes place in the uppermost layers of the materials, helps to even out the room climate, and is very much wanted. Some building materials, like brick, lime, chalk, plaster, and wood, are better suited than others to be moisture buffers, like glass, metal, plastic, concrete and painted surfaces. In rooms with sealed surfaces, greater air dampness concentrations can be expected. Concrete surfaces almost completely prevent absorption.

# Ventilation Principles

In small cellars the principle of free natural ventilation can be used effectively. It is based on the convection behavior of the air. Warmer, damper air is lighter than cooler air and thus rises in the room.

*Natural air circulation by ventilation chimneys—more or less well maintained!*

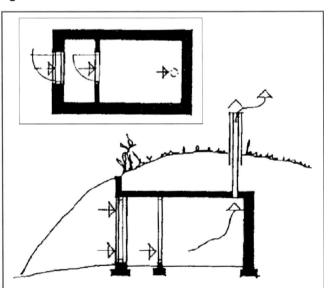

If it is a small room with just one window, the intake and exhaust pipes can both be led through it.

**Example:** Nomads use a porous container of water, on which a filter with charcoal is placed in the middle of an air intake for cooling air. The warm air lets the water evaporate and the room is cooled.

In free natural cellar ventilation, both the temperature and the humidity conditions are controlled by the installation of intake and outflow air channels with adjustable openings. Cold air is conducted in from outside. This usually takes place through a shaft or pipe that runs several meters underground. The air is cooled more by increasing the pipe length and is conducted into the room from below. The air is warmed in the cellar and thus can take up excess humidity, becomes lighter, and rises. This warm, humid air is conducted out, under ideal conditions, at the highest point in the room. By rising, it draws the cooler air from the lower opening after it. Thus, at different temperatures, an air exchange between inside and outside can be attained.

To assume the functioning of this simple and, above all, reasonably priced ventilation principle, one must make sure of certain criteria: The intake opening for the outside air must be on the north side and as much in the shade as possible. The air exchange is increased if the departing air leaves through a chimney. The room is then under low pressure. The air speed becomes greater as the shaft is lengthened. Wind on the outflow opening can increase the air change considerably. If the outflow shaft (such as a stainless steel chimney) is open to sunlight, thermal forces do the rest. The intake and outflow openings should be placed on opposite sides if possible. The air intake should enter on a wide surface.

It is best to make the air openings large and then regulate the ventilation by means of adjustable slides.

Free natural ventilation, as already noted, depends on many mutually influential factors for its effectiveness.

If cooling by light-air ventilation does not work, one can always use a pressure system and intake ventilator for fresh-air cooling, or mechanical cooling by means of a cooling system or vaporizer.

THE SLIDERS MUST BE INSULATED TO KEEP OUT WARMTH! ATTACH SCREENS TO KEEP OUT INSECTS!

AIR SHAFTS MUST BE KEPT OPEN AND NOT SWITCHED!

## WARMTH PROTECTION

Warmth insulation has the task of decreasing the transmission of warmth between inside and outside. Through the proper warmth-insulation measures in the wine cellar, one can avoid structural defects leading to adverse conditions such as water condensation and mold formation. One may also prevent great tension on load-bearing structures by eliminating winter cooling and summer heating of structural elements that enclose the room.

With temperature differences inside and outside, one strives for temperature equalization. The warmth always flows from the warmer place to the cooler one until equalization is accomplished.

Therefore cold penetrates into the building in winter and warmth in summer.

*Warm insulation on the outside wall must succeed completely so that no cold bridges can arise, nor the condensation surfaces on the inside walls where mold will form.*

An important comparison value is the U-value (formerly k-value). It is a measure of the warmth penetration through a building component and is stated in $W/(m^2 K)$. Thus the U-value expresses what performance is needed per square meter on one side of the component to maintain a temperature difference of one Kelvin.

From this it is derived that the conductive capability of a material is greater the thicker, heavier, and damper it is, and the fewer pores it has.

Accordingly, there are good and bad heat conductors. Light, porous materials like insulation are poor conductors; thick, heavy masses like concrete or metal scarcely offer any resistance to the flow of warmth. Therefore, insulation is usually light.

A good heat insulator is air; the best would be a vacuum, which cuts off the energy transport from molecule to molecule. Water, on the other hand, conducts 25 times better than air! If water penetrates into building materials, especially insulation, the insulating value is decreased considerably. Thus, a seal before open-pored insulation, or ventilation from the rear is needed.

In the evaluation of building materials, though, how much warmth they let through is not so important, but rather how much they prevent the heat flow, thus how much they insulate. The comparison value is called warmth passage resistance and characterizes the heat-insulating ability of a material.

But it is not only the characteristics of insulation materials, and their sufficient strength, that are important, but also their correct constructive application. Cold or heat bridges must be avoided.

A cold bridge exists when temperature differences occur between inside and outside. In practice, that happens when the warmth insulation is not applied without gaps.

The room temperatures of unheated cellars depend on what materials the cellar is built of and how deep in the ground it is, or whether adjoining rooms are heated or not. In the winter it is comparatively warm in the cellar compared to outdoors, in the summer, cool. In a cellar that is very well insulated, particularly in the ceiling, the air temperature of the cellar will more or less reach that of the adjoining ground. When the cellar ceiling is poorly insulated, the air temperature of the cellar will equal that of the heated ground-floor rooms. But other warmth-insulating measures can be considered during planning. Also of importance are the situation of the cellar and its relation of the outdoor surfaces to the volume of the building.

MATERIALS WITH GOOD WARMTH-INSULATION QUALITIES HAVE A POOR ABILITY TO CONDUCT WARMTH!

IN CASE COLD BRIDGES CANNOT BE ELIMINATED COMPLETELY, THE HUMIDITY OF THE AIR MUST BE DECREASED AS A CAUTIONARY MEASURE.

BUILDINGS USED TO VENTILATE THEMSELVES. AIR PUSHED IN THROUGH COUNTLESS SPACES AND CRACKS.

# Locations and Possibilities for Wine Storage

An old saying:
"The cellar makes the wine!"

The word "cellar" comes from Latin. The *"cellarium"* was then a storage room or a food pantry. The cellar was usually partly or for the most part underground. It was cool in the summer and frost-free in the winter, and served to store fresh fruits and vegetables.

Formerly the cellar was—as said—primarily a cool, damp storage room for food and wine. Later, heating and fuel storage were housed in the cellar. Thus, the cellar became warm and dry. It was thereby ideal for a hobby and storage room. But it was thus robbed of its true function as a food-storage place.

For storing wine, a cool, dry, odor-neutral natural cellar is probably the most ideal place. If one has no such cellar, one can naturally also adapt an existing cellar as a wine cellar. But the cellar should at least be dry, not overheated, and dark.

## Vaulted Cellars

The classic wine cellar is an underground cellar, usually a vaulted cellar. Almost all of them were

A traditional wine-storage cellar in a country house near Graz

formerly built as storage places for wooden barrels, and they usually had a good room climate. They were evenly cool and moist, and that was depended on.

Arches are the oldest forms of massive ceilings. Along with the walls of the building, they form a firm structure. The building of arches requires some experience and understanding. For as far as their form is concerned, they are built only to support load pressures. House cellars usually had an arch with a cylindrical arch surface as a ceiling—a barrel-shaped arch rather than a pointed arch, which allowed a better use of the room's height. These ceilings were divided into small arches by pillars. In old houses, there were often carved cellars of natural stone, or arches of stone and brick. The floors consisted of stamped soil or natural stone plates.

The farther down in the ground the cellar is, the more even the temperature in an arched cellar is. The principle is that the temperature progression in the ground is displaced in phases. That means the deeper in the ground a cellar is, the more time-displaced the influence of the surface temperature is on the temperature of the structure in the ground. But the room temperatures of such cellars also depend on what material the cellars were made of, and whether adjoining rooms are heated or not. Usually, the temperatures vary be-

*New splendor in an old hut (above); Inviting: traditional cupola cellar; Lamprecht, Kloech (below)*

Arched cellars are valuable inheritances today, but they are seldom built new, because their building is expensive and their care is troublesome.

*Architecturally valuable and physically well-maintained belted arch*

IN EXISTING VAULTED CELLARS, RISING MOISTURE OFTEN CAUSES HARM TO ROOMS ABOVE. DRYNESS AND DAMPNESS MUST BE SEPARATED FROM EACH OTHER BY ISOLATION.

tween 10 and 18 degrees. In extreme cases, with very good insulation of the cellar ceiling, the air temperature in the cellar approximately equals the temperature of the adjoining soil. In the reverse case—with strong insulation of the cellar walls and floor—the air temperature of the cellar will resemble the temperature of the heated ground-floor rooms. Drawing on next page.

If vaulted cellars are too dry, bricks are a suitable floor material. Their surface can be dampened to a degree.

So that the dampness of the cellar could not rise into the ground floor, high foundations were formerly built, so that the ceiling of the cellar was above ground level. Thus, sufficient evaporation surfaces were present, since the cellar was constantly ventilated via open window shafts. Later horizontal insulation was built into the outside walls, but the cellar floor remained constantly damp at first.

If such a cellar is extended later, thick plaster is used or new, tightly closing windows are installed. The evaporation of the moisture on the surfaces no longer takes place then, and moisture damage is programmed in advance.

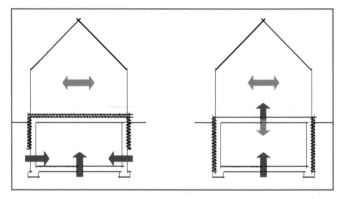

# EARTHEN CELLARS

BECAUSE OF THE USUALLY HIGH DAMPNESS, EARTHEN CELLARS SHOULD ALWAYS BE BUILT APART FROM THE DWELLING HOUSE!

Earthen cellars sometime solve the problem of holding the supplies where houses lack suitable cellars. Reinforced concrete cellars are initially well suited as storage cellars—because of the great dampness of the materials. But when this moisture] has evaporated, this effect is also gone.

**Exception:** A lime soil can be watered artificially, but that can cause damage to the main house.

Earthen cellars usually have an arch made of bricks or old rubble, stretching all the way from the foundation. Check the stability of old bricks! Do not use any damaged or deteriorating bricks!

To keep the temperature difference between inside and outside as low as possible, a great mass of material is needed. Thus, the earth covering must be sufficient. The thickness depends on the sunlight and the insulation. Thus, the entrances to earthen cellars were usually located on the north or shady side.

An additional insulation of fiberglass may turn out to be necessary. Fiberglass is hard, bears a load, and can also be regarded as biologically positive.

An external insulation prevents roots from growing in. This insulation can be made of chalk or Trass mortar or a normal spackled seal. Runoff water then gathers in a channel of rubble and thus—if necessary—waters the lime soil. Increasing moisture is the best watering.

Dip old bricks in water so the mortar does not set so quickly.

The soil should be as open as possible and, for added moisturizing, be fitted with an open gutter with a hose (inside drainage).

*A neat entrance to an earthen cellar is built on the shady side and overgrown with bushes*

The ventilation shaft should be set atop the arch. Clay pipe is a compromise that roots can grow through easily. The best is a masonry shaft that is not insulated. But ventilation shafts made of galvanized or coated metal or stainless steel are also suitable.

With an earthen cellar in a dwelling house, the floor paving is cut out where the natural cellar is to be placed. The floor should be at least 50 cm deeper here than the upper edge of the other parts of the cellar, so that a layer of cold air exists in the lowered area. To increase the moisture in the air, it is recommended that bricks be laid on a sand bed on the concrete floor, and moistened with water now and then. When an earthen cellar is installed, one must be clear as to what is to be stored in it.

**Attention:** This also applies to the air ducting!

Much moisture must be kept outside of a wine cellar; but it should come into an earthen cellar! Earthen cellars are thus better suited for storing fruits and vegetables.

## Conventional Cellar Buildings

Concrete is the most frequently used construction material of newly built cellars.

To attain a dry cellar, it must be protected sufficiently from moisture in the ground, rising ground water, and oppressive wetness. The cellar must also have good insulation from warmth, so that no moisture from the air condenses on the cold cellar walls.

To deal with the frequent situation in which, for example, water running down a slope pushes against a cellar wall and threatens to destroy it, simple drainage helps, and can be added later when repairing structural damage. The soil is removed down to the bottom and the open space is filled with coarse gravel. A special drainage pipe makes sure that collecting water is channeled off into the canalization or into a drainage ditch. An

*Do not forget walkways and floor attachments for shelves!*

*Do not store fruits and vegetables along with wine! Wine can stand much less moisture in the air that fruits and vegetables require.*

*Sealing materials should always be outside, where warmth or coldness arrives, so as not to subject building components to needless tension and avoid warm or cold bridges.*

*Whether made of ready-made components or fresh-poured concrete—protection from incoming moisture by a sealed strip (above) or bituminous paint (below) is essential.*

indestructible synthetic sheet assures that the gravel does not settle too far into the soil. Concrete cellar walls must be sealed and made watertight.

This is done with a tar coating and a watertight layer extending down into the ground. This should be made stronger above ground, on the south side, and in the area of a flat roof.

Cooling cannot be accomplished with insulating materials, but the penetration of either warmth or coldness from outside can be slowed.

**Attention:** There are specific sealing materials for use above and below ground level! Many insulators against warmth absorb moisture when used incorrectly. If this moisture, once taken in, cannot get out again, the insulating effect is lowered or even destroyed.

For safety's sake, attach an evaporation shield on the inside of the room and ventilate the warm insulation behind it.

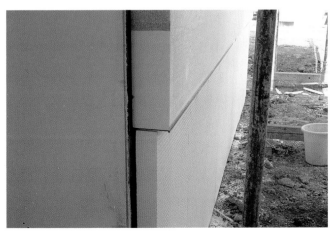

*Careful insulation reduces the cold bridges and thus the condensation surfaces inside.*

# Cellars in Houses

The room is sealed with tar. A brick wall is installed at an interval of 5 cm. Drainage ducts are installed behind it as internal drainage for artificial dampening, without endangering rooms on the floor above.

Avoid shaking caused by stairway use!

In a standard cellar, one cannot attain an ideal storage climate without small-scale adaptations. A wine-storage cellar should be insulated from warmer living areas. Very often a separate cellar room serves not only for wine storage, but can also house many other treasures. As long as the storage conditions for foods and such are similar to those for wine, there is no objection to mutual storage. But the room will then not be suitable as a wine cellar as well as a food storage place. With the same construction, and if the size is sufficient, the free space under the stairs offers several possibilities for optimal use, since this space is generally not heated and often remains totally unused otherwise. With some skill, a usable and nice wine cellar can be set up, even in a very small space.

The presence of hot water pipes running through the cellar also causes temperatures to rise. Thus, they should also be insulated. In an ideal case, the storage location should be placed far away from any possible source of warmth (such as central heating), be on the north side, and be easy to ventilate. In reinforced concrete cellars there can also be exceptional cases in which the cellar area is too dry.

*Wine and other foods can be stored together*

# Cellars in Outbuildings

Building a wine cellar in or under an unused outbuilding is a good solution. The possibilities range from an underground vaulted cellar to a ground-level cooling room.

# Cooling Rooms

Even if one cannot erect a cellar in his house or apartment, there are possibilities for installing a wine cellar. One insulates a closet, storage space or small room.

By means of cooling systems, this area can be kept at a constant temperature. If this much space is not sufficient, then a cellar area can be rebuilt into a cooling room by installing insulation and air conditioning. Then constant conditions, optimal for wine storage, can prevail. This variation makes the perfect storage for every wine possible.

# Rented Cellars

Some vintners also rent their customers private, locked areas and shelves. Here wine fans can store

*Unmistakable: Traditional cellar entrance*

*Controlled storage conditions, also for large quantities of wine*

*Rented cellar: Entry only for users*

*Locking rented spaces*

their personal wines in ideal conditions, sample them, and take them hone for use.

The usual household refrigerator is entirely unsuitable for wine storage. It undergoes shaking and temperature variations.

## Wine Climate Cabinets

If one does not have one's own wine cellar, or if space with ideal storage conditions is lacking to set up a wine cellar in the house, then one should obtain a wine climate cabinet. This is a refrigerator developed especially for the storage of wine. The storage capacity, depending on the model, goes up to 200 bottles on adjustable shelves. Wine climate cabinets, unlike typical refrigerators, run completely without vibrations and have air filters to prevent mold formation.

Built-in forced-air cooling provides sufficient moisture and an even temperature. The possible temperature-setting area is between 2 and 15 degrees C. Wine climate cabinets either have their own self-chosen temperature zone or several temperature areas.

If one wants to let one's wines be stored and mature over long periods, then a climate cabinet with one temperature zone is especially suitable. The worthiness of the wines should in every case be compared with the cost of the energy.

Nicely integrated, and clearly visible with standing wine storage

Wine climate cabinets as temperature-controlled showcases are especially practical in the living area—no matter whether one has a wine cellar or not. The most refined showcases have sections with different temperature areas, in which white and red wines can be kept at the right temperature, so that one is no longer in a quandary at an unexpected visit!

1A climate cabinet with two or three temperature areas is ideal: 4-9 degrees C for white and sparkling wines, 10-15 degrees for the storage and maturing of white and red wines, 14-18 degrees for red wines ready to drink. Besides the factual and visible aspects, when you buy such a wine climate cabinet, note the technical details and energy needs as well!

# Storage Systems

Wine cabinets serve primarily to store bottles in an organized, visible manner, and particularly as best for the wine. Every wine must be easy to find, if possible without moving other bottles. Shelves and racks must be stable and easy to reach, and should, if possible, have various divisions. Large sections and shelves on which many bottles are stored one above the other require, in turn, large numbers of one type of wine. More practical and useful for the private wine cellar are shelves and racks in varying sizes that offer space for about a dozen or fewer bottles of the same wine, as well as single bottles (such as magnums).

**Do not fill the entire wine-storage space with shelves. One also needs free surfaces for placing and unpacking, as well as for temporary storage of new acquisitions.**

In this chapter there is a broad spectrum of suggested means of storing wine visibly.

Important criteria in the choice of suitable shelves are stability, structure, material, size, and shape.

### Liability
The examples shown in the book are strictly system sketches. The dimensions of the designs are not based on exact considerations of material, attachment, number, and weight of bottles, construction of the space (wall and ceiling design) or statics.

# Bottles:
# Shapes and Stacking Possibilities

If one assumes from the start that bottles are stored lying down as a rule, then several possible

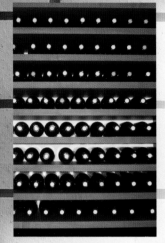

Bottles: Shapes and
Stacking Possibilities

forms of stacking exist. Decisive for them are the shape of the bottle, as well as the fact that almost every bottle has its own dimensions (length, diameter, weight). Naturally there is also a norm by which the glass-blowing works produce their bottles of certain capacities. The individual wishes and requirements, though, have naturally led to a very great variety, which in turn does not allow a general statement about the dimensions of the storage spaces. Bottles that hold a certain amount are marked with a backward "E" on the bottom or the bottom seam. In addition, one finds the brim volumes without a statement of the unit of measurement in centiliters, or with the volume in millimeters from the upper rim of the bottle (such as "77" or "30 mm"), the specified volume in liters, centiliters or milliliters (such as 0.75 l, 75 cm, 750 ml), plus the federal government's mark of the glass factory for sealing and measuring uses.

*Statement of the specified volume and filling height on the bottom of a definite-volume bottle...*

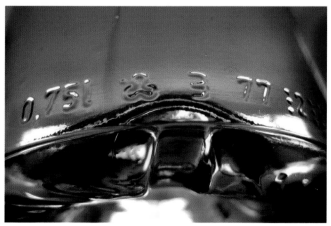

*...or at the bottom seam (750 ml specified volume at 770 mm rim volume)*

To provide a starting point for the dimensions of your wine-storage system, we have tried to combine the most common bottle types in a table. From the data of diameter, height and dry weight, cabinets for storing bottles can be dimensioned and designed individually, which is especially important for the stability of the system. For the carrying power, the weight of the valuable contents must naturally be added—the relative gravity of wine is about 1.0000, which means that 750 liters equal 750 grams—and then correspondingly over-dimensioned.

Styria    Bordeaux    Burgundy    Rhine Wine

## Measurements of Common Bottle Types

|  | 0.375 l | 0.5 l | 0.75 l | 1.5 l (magnum) |
|---|---|---|---|---|
| Top Bordeaux | -/-/- | 65.5/267.5/368 | 73.9/340/641 | -/-/- |
| Bordeaux 400 | 62.5/246/340 | -/-/- | 76/289/400 | 83.5/346/690 |
| Bordeaux Exclusive | 61.5/251/350 | -/-/- | 76.2/300.5/500 | -/-/- |
| Bordeaux Europa | -/-/- | -/-/- | 76/316/600 | -/-/- |
| Bordeaux Prestige | -/-/- | -/-/- | 75.4/300/500 | -/-/- |
| Bordeaux 310 | -/-/- | -/-/- | 75.1/310.460 | -/-/- |
| Bordeaux BA | 61/280/478 | -/-/- | -/-/- | -/-/- |
| Bordolese | -/-/- | -/-/- | 75.7/293/410 | -/-/- |
| Bordolese Europea | -/-/- | -/-/- | 75.3/316/560 | -/-/- |
| Bordolese Futura | -/-/- | 61.7/353/600 | -/-/- | -/-/- |
|  |  |  |  |  |
| Burgundy Medium | -/-/- | -/-/- | 80.5/282/400 | -/-/- |
| Burgundy Wine | 66/246.5/373 | -/-/- | 81.6/278/425 | 106/348/870 |
| Burgundy Tradition F | -/-/- | -/-/- | 82/296/573 | -/-/- |
| Burgundy Exclusive | -/-/- | -/-/- | 81/296/500 | -/-/- |
|  |  |  |  |  |
| Styria | -/-/- | 64.2/289/405 | 73/330/540 | -/-/- |
|  |  |  |  |  |
| Rhine Wine | 61.5/274.5/355 | 64.2/289/405 | 75.7/328/440 | -/-/- |
| Rhine Exclusive 500 | -/-/- | -/-/- | 77.9/350/500 | -/-/- |
| Rhine Prestige | -/-/- | -/-/- | 78.1/353/550 | -/-/- |

Source: www.vetropack.at                              (diameter/height/weight)

In calculating the bottle sizes, it depends on the manner in which one wants to arrange the bottles. Depending on the bottle shape, three different basic types have been defined by us. For bottles with a straight body form (Styria, Bordeaux), all three types are possible. For wedge-shaped bottles (Burgundy, Rhine wine), only stacking type two is recommended, for when they are stacked high, a push can cause them to tip.

Stacking type three is possible only for two to three layers of Burgundy and Rhine wine since the stack would collapse into itself without support from spacers.

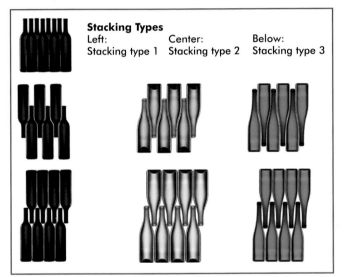

**Stacking Types**
Left:                     Center:                     Below:
Stacking type 1   Stacking type 2   Stacking type 3

Along with the bottle shape and the resulting stacking type, the measurements of the bottles in particular are interesting, since the size (width, depth, and height) of the spaces depends on them. If the space is not matched to the bottle size, spacers in the form of wedges or wooden pieces are necessary to attain proper stability. For the optimal space width and height, two forms of measurement result, in which the diameter of the bottle is taken as "n" and the number of bottles per space with "X".

A. X times n with positions exactly over each other and full use of the width (Sketch 1).

B. X times n/2 with the upper layer stacked in the spaces of the lower layer (Sketch 2).

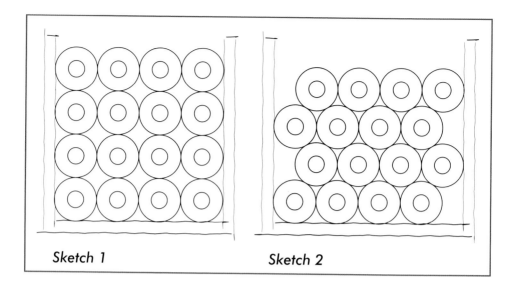

Sketch 1                              Sketch 2

Along with the common 0.75-liter bottles, there are smaller formats for individual use, and for special wines of certain vintages, large bottles with capacities of up to 40 liters. There are particularly champagne bottles that, with the exceptions of Primat and Souverain, bear biblical names with stories behind them.

| Normal Size | Liters | Name |
|---|---|---|
| ¼ | 0.2 | Piccolo |
| ½ | 0.375 | Demi/Filette |
| 1 | 0.75 | Imperial |
| 2 | 1.5 | Magnum |
| 4 | 3 | Jeroboam/Double Magnum |
| 6 | 4.5 | Rehoboam |
| 8 | 6 | Methusalem |
| 12 | 9 | Salmanzar |
| 16 | 12 | Balthazar |
| 20 | 15 | Nebuchadnezar |
| 24 | 18 | Melchior or Goliath |
| 35 | 26.25 | Souverain or Sovereign |
| 36 | 27 | Primat |
| 40 | 39 | Melchizidek |

*Large bottles have collectors' and also decorative values*

# Storage in the Original Packing

Wine packed in wooden crates is very decorative. It can also be stored when thus packed, which protects the bottles from dust and the much-feared cork moth.

The crates should not stand directly on the floor, but be stored on wooden blocks, completely surrounded by air.

Whoever does not want to store his wine in the original wooden crates should still keep them. When one sells, they reassure the buyer and increase the value of the wine. This is especially true of magnums and other large bottles.

As gifts too, wines in wooden crates appear more decorative and valuable.

Cardboard cartons are generally used only for temporary storage, since they grow moldy at too-high humidity (over 35%) and can thus transmit odors and rot. In addition, they then lose stability. Under optimal storage conditions, cartons made especially for the purpose also offer the possibility of long-term storage.

*Check the bottles now and then.*

*Orderly and stable storage in wooden crates*

# Commercial Shelving Systems

The trade offers variable, stackable stone or interlocking systems made of all possible materials. They can be combined in many ways and are decorative. There are scarcely any limits to their individual formative possibilities.

The building stones can easily be combined to form stable and high shelves, and are available in various sizes and shapes.

Usually there are special parts, like wrought iron or glass doors, wine cabinets for special bodies, special components, and much more.

*Not made for the job, and yet functional office shelving*

| **Advantages** | easy to erect |
| --- | --- |
| | easy to expand |
| | most varied possible shapes |
| | easy to fit into the space |
| | many special elements |
| | good wine climate |
| | easy to see the wine |
| | good space utilization |
| **Disadvantages** | expensive |
| | not individual—uniform |

# Homemade Shelves

Bean-eater, Phantom of the Opera, Starfighter or Wide World, Billy, Sultan, Knut, Astro, Barbara, Catch Me, Black is Black ... and all the rest.

Based on the names of more or less well-known wines and furniture from renowned furnishing firms, we have also let our imagination play games and given names to our creations!

On the underside one can attach rubber pads to dampen vibration.

Homemade shelves can also be made of wood, metal, bricks or natural stone. Because of the weight of the bottles, they must be firmly attached to the wall or ceiling. So the cellar air can circulate, the shelves should be some 5 cm from the wall, floor and ceiling. The bases of the shelves should be made of metal or hardwood and their height should be adjustable, so they can even out unevenness of the floor. Individual cabinets with special wines can also be lockable and fitted with wooden doors with air holes, metal grids or glass. Dividers are especially practical. They divide the shelf into smaller units and keep the bottles stable.

*Homemade wine racks with roof lattice—uncomplicated and practical (left)*

*Lock-up section for especially valuable bottles (right)*

---

**There are no good or bad materials, but only rightly or wrongly used or installed materials.**

---

# Examples Made of Brick

## Materials and Characteristics

The brick is not only one of the oldest building materials, but also one of the most important, because of its versatility and technically good qualities.

Bricks are ceramic building materials made of clay. The rough material is pressed, dried, and baked at about 1000 degrees C. Thus a porous structure results. If bricks are baked over 1000 degrees, the pores close and the surface becomes glassy. Thus, the frost-fast clinker brick is formed, which is used, for example, for decorative brickwork or floor paving.

History: Bricks were formerly baked in piles; thus the color differences from black to blue came into being.

Bricks are very advantageous for the natural wine climate.

The size of a typical brick is 25 x 12 x 6.5 cm.

*Rustic and pleasant: used bricks and massive wooden furniture*

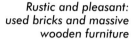

*Secret "safe" (above)
Open secret (below)*

**Advantages:**    high pressure-resistance
good heat storage
equalizes moisture, breathes
   actively
fire-resistant
secure from mold and decay
resistant to vermin
resistant to chemical influences
easy to work with
lasting, maintain their shape
local building materials
pleasant room climate

**Disadvantages:**  high weight
damp from mortar
clinker bricks can be
   diffusion-impervious

### "Stone Upon Stone"

For many, the classic wine shelves are those built solely of bricks. Brick has a tradition, is stable, looks good, and is physically very easy to maintain.

Bricks are most often used in their usual form. It is handy and forms pleasant patterns, depending on the depth and formation of the shelves.

When bricks are used—as here—as the only material, the base of the shelves must be made slightly arched to support the weight. The bricks can then be used either lying or standing. Depending

Clinker bricks: sharp angles (left)

Used bricks provide harmony (right)

on the shelf depth, the bottles can be stored according to various manners of stacking.

Old bricks look especially good because of their color effects. The color variations arise during baking from the varying mixture of raw materials and the varying temperatures of the baking process.

If one has no old bricks available, one can naturally use new ones. They should not, though, be artificially trimmed to look old, such as by knocking off corners.

To be sure, clinker bricks, such as are often used outdoors for facades or ground pavement, can also be used. Because of their higher baking temperature, they are harder, but also denser than typical bricks.

The combination of the materials here is especially important. The higher the chalk content and the lower the cement content, the higher the breathing activity.

For simple shelf patterns, single levels can also be fitted with doors. Opaque doors protect valuable bottles from curious looks (such as in cellars and multi-family houses).

In addition, other "unrelated" drink bottles, like those of fruit juices or cider, can also be kept hidden away in a cool wine cellar. Wood and metal are most suitable as materials, but so is satinized or colored glass. Don't forget to provide air holes!

Transparent doors can be made of simple grids, but also of wrought iron patterns. Here not only the motif of the grid but also the bottles behind them, especially if illuminated, will create an atmosphere.

### "The Treasure of Silver Mountain"

An optimal variant in utilizing bricks is their use in combination with another material.

The brick is used as the load-bearing element of the shelves. The shelf bases, however, are made partly of wood, glass or metal. In these shelves, the vertical lines are especially emphasized. The horizontal shelf bottoms can be made correspondingly thinner and lighter, and thereby recede into the background. (Sketch 1)

This shelf variant can also be combined effectively with arches, or even be fitted into arch spaces.

If the shelf bases are held by metal pins, the individual brick walls do not have to be built up exactly equal. The metal pins can be inserted in the mortar or the bricks. (Sketch 4)

Regardless of the fact that pins may be inserted into brick or mortar, the appearance is far more elegant, and seems far more exactly built, when the shelves fit into slots of the same height in the brick face. When the shelf bottoms can be fitted directly into the mortar joints, needing no extra support with appropriate mounting, this look is achieved.

In an ideal case, all slots are made equally deep. This gives the advantage that the shelf bottoms can be adjusted in height as one wishes and are suited to rising or dwindling stocks.

Wood, for example, is suitable as a material for the shelving. Here, of course, one must keep in mind that the wooden board or the laminated plate must have a certain constructive height to be able to hold the weight of the bottles. Otherwise, the shelves no longer look so graceful, and the slots also have to be made appropriately strong. To avoid this, one can also install the last brick below the shelf bottom on edge and thus use the space as a site for the wooden bottom. In this form, of course, rearrangement of the shelf height is no longer possible. (Sketch 3)

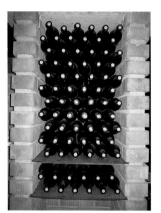

*Variable shelf heights through double functioning of the joints*

Glass is a good alternative as a shelf bottom, especially reinforced glass. To be sure, this possibility can only be recommended for light loads. With heavy loads, cracks can result. The shelf does not break through the inlaid wire, but does not look very good. A combination of glass with a metal frame has proven best. (Sketch 5) The frame is pushed into the slots. The glass plate is somewhat less wide and lies freely above it within the carrier construction.

*Fixed shelf heights are created when installing a wooden base upon projecting bricks*

If one uses one brick per shelf completely instead of half, the result is a small projection on which a single bottle can be placed decoratively. (Sketch 2) This is especially recommended for large numbers of one type. The single bottle indicates the contents of that shelf or section.

This shelving system is usable as a space divider. It can be built up with single, double or balanced stacking processes.

The shelf bottom, though, does not always have to be made horizontal. Whoever likes "diagonals" can include them in the quadrilateral pattern.

*Larger areas can be divided simply and practically*

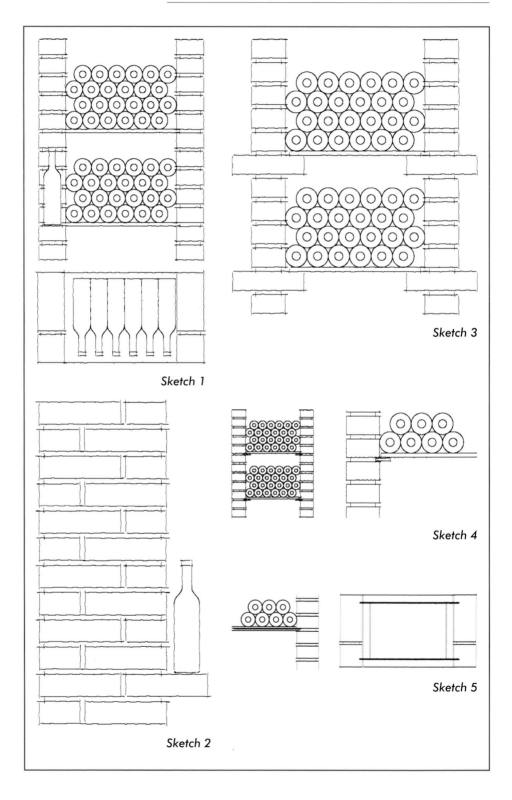

Sketch 1

Sketch 2

Sketch 3

Sketch 4

Sketch 5

## "1, 2... Cornerstone, All Must Be Hidden"

This shelf variant differs from the previous one in its type of surface formation. Here the bricks are not shown, but disappear under a layer of plaster. This possibility is especially suitable for small spaces. The light surface of the plaster then makes the room appear to be bigger. The same, by the way, applies to the floor and ceiling. The bricks can also be plastered over if they no longer make such a good appearance; damaged places may be hidden by plaster, or if one has only new bricks available and does not want them to show. The shelf can even be built of a completely different material and the "bricks" only imitated. Of course this is not completely right, but it cannot be seen at first glance. This applies, for example, to the use of Ytong, wood or wood-based materials that are plastered or only spackled and painted.

If dividers are needed, the choice of materials is not so difficult. Almost any color will do. Since the brick joints of plastered, shelf walls are not visible, the strength of the inlaid floor need be chosen only according to the static requirements. Thus, even several centimeters of wooden boards can be used. Dark boards in particular make a nice contrast to the white carrier walls. And, naturally, it is also permissible to color the plaster!

With this shelf system, though, existing window and door frames, as well as existing niches, can simply be rebuilt into wine shelves.

*If spaces are very low, making the ceiling a light color is recommended.*

*Decorative, though technically not right*

*Tasting spaces are usually too warm for wine storage*

It is just as important to make sure that the wine is not exposed to too much sunlight or for too long.

For very small niches, in exceptional cases, the wines can also be stored standing. Here decorative bottles with nice labels are very effective. They can even be empty and be kept in remembrance of a tasty drop or a special occasion.

Nice effects can also be achieved when individual bricks or even arch elements are highlighted with paint.

If one type of wine leaks out, minor stains can easily be hidden by paint!

WITH ARCHES, THE ARCH ITSELF
CAN BE LEFT UNPLASTERED
WHILE THE ARCH FIELDS
ARE PLASTERED.

Niches in walls are especially suitable for wine storage

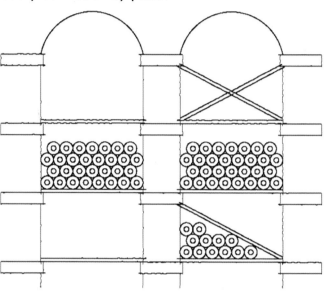

## "Urbanus"

In this kind of wine shelf, the brick walls are broken several times by horizontal wooden shelves.

The horizontal element is stressed. The shelves look secure and "substantial."

Very tall, narrow spaces can be made to look lower by stressing the width. (Sketch 1)

As for the material itself, one can plaster the bricks or leave them uncovered. Since the wood is accented particularly here, the use of native woods with striking veining, such as walnut or oak, is recommended.

The full-width wooden boards can be worked into the shelf front evenly or projecting forward.

The latter variant is ideal for storing bottles and glasses or keeping a cellar book. (Sketch 2)

Whoever wants to can also make the lower part of his shelves deeper than the upper part. Then, for example, bottles can even be stacked unevenly. (Sketch 4) A further possibility is to store wooden or metal crates on rollers at the bottom. Other drinks, packing materials or other wine bottles can be stored in them. (Sketch 5)

In this variant, the section sizes are more or less fixed. Various widths can be built in during construction. (Sketch 3) In terms of height, though, they cannot be varied, which makes the shelves look very uniform. If one really wants to divide a section, this can be done easily with a diagonal board.

*Easy-to-see sections with numbers and symbolic bottles in front*

The shelves can reach from floor to ceiling.

As for the upper closing of the shelves, there are two possibilities. If no closing wooden plate is laid on the last brick, the shelves look lighter and the transition to the ceiling is not so hard.

If the closing is done with one last full-width wooden plate, the shelves appear to be framed. Then too, the resulting structure appears especially good for storing empty boxes or wine bottles in wooden crates.

IN CASES of REAL ARCHES, differently ARCHED CEILINGS — SUCH AS TRAVERSE ENDS AND WOODEN CEILINGS — OR EVEN LOW CEILINGS, IT IS RECOMMENDED NOT TO EXTEND THE WINE SHELVES RIGHT UP UNDER THE CEILING.

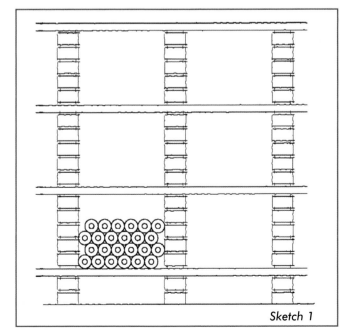

*Sketch 1*

*The shelf height should be within everyone's reach*

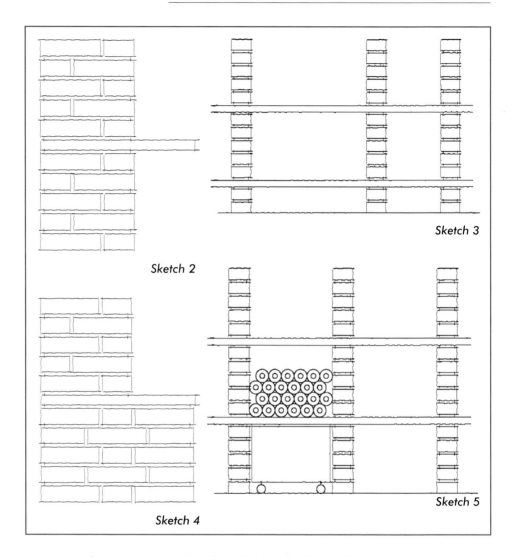

Sketch 2

Sketch 3

Sketch 4

Sketch 5

### "Fixed and Finished Bricks"
### Wine-storage Brick Elements and
### Clay Cylinders

The carefully chosen wines deserve a special, elegant storage place. The natural product of clay, because of its physical characteristics, offers the wine the best conditions for storage. In this system several forms of clay components are available and can also be combined with each other to form the most varied forms and structures. The material protects the bottles from light and simultaneously forms a friendly, homey picture. Each bottle is sepa-

*Clay cylinders are built up quickly and simply...*

rate, which is especially advantageous for stacking bottles of Rhine wine (mallet bottles) and Burgundy and allows independence in storing bottles of different sizes. The system can be built up very simply and quickly, needs no additional components or work processes to attain stability, and can form an impressive optical pattern. One disadvantage is surely that labels cannot be seen, which leads to frequent movement when seeking a bottle. Thus the needed rest of the wine is disturbed. A label on the neck of the bottle can help.

### Tʜᴇ U-sʜᴀᴘᴇᴅ Wɪɴᴇ Sʜᴇʟᴠᴇs

Surface needed: 11.5 pieces per square meter (without free space to install shelf bottom). The length of 30 cm corresponds to a standard 1-liter wine bottle or a long 0.75-liter wine bottle.

*... and can be designed individually*

### Tʜᴇ 6-ʜᴏʟᴇ Wɪɴᴇ-ᴄᴇʟʟᴀʀ Bʟᴏᴄᴋ

Surface needed: 11.5 pieces per square meter (without free space to install shelf bottom). Using grooves on all four sides, shelf bottoms up to a thickness of 2 cm can be installed in the desired height.

### Tʜᴇ 9-ʜᴏʟᴇ Wɪɴᴇ-ᴄᴇʟʟᴀʀ Bʟᴏᴄᴋ

Surface needed: 8.7 pieces per square meter (without free space to install shelf bottom). With grooves on both sides, shelf bottoms up to a thickness of 2.5 centimeters can be installed in the desired height.

### The Wine-shelf Tile Ornament

Surface needed: 18 pieces per square meter (without free space to install shelf bottom).

### The Bocksbeutel Wine-cellar Tile

Surface needed: 18 pieces per square meter.
These wine-cellar tiles can also be combined with wooden boards to make a set of shelves. Unfortunately, this system needs a fair amount of space. In addition, it does not allow a good view. If one wants to know what a wine is, one must move the wine bottle, unless it is easy to see (for instance, by the bottle neck). Shelves of drainage pipes can be mounted in mortar or plastered in place.

| | |
|---|---|
| **Advantages** | Actively breathing material |
| **Disadvantages** | Needs much space |
| | Does not offer a good view |
| | Bottles must be moved |

### Hydro-clay

For the most part, the "hydro-clay" shelf consists of inflated clay, also known as "Leca" (lightweight expanded clay aggregates). This is ground out of chalk-poor clay, granulated and burned, and has the ability to absorb moisture and give it off again. This system is also easy and, because of the form of the basic elements, has sufficient stability. It can be fitted optimally to the needs of your wine collection. Easy to see and practical, it offers a place for your individual wine rarities as well as all fifty bottles of your "favorite wine." The bottles lie in bottle-sized grooves absolutely free from rolling. The shelf bottoms can be had in 60 mm and 99 mm widths. The spaces between the shelves can be varied by means of the supporting side pieces.

*Hydro-clay shelves can be set up individually!*

As an optically striking crown, an arcade can be made on top out of two arched elements.

For bottles that are better stored standing, such as Tokay, one simply uses the shelf bottoms with the flat side upward. The basic elements are made in light Bordeaux red and thus fit into any surroundings. The height-stability and flexibility can be regarded as a decisive advantage of this system. It is simple to build and can be expanded at any time. There are also a number of components that, on the one hand, allow an individual style, and on the other, clearly improve the visibility.

## Examples Made of Natural Stone

### Materials and Characteristics

Natural stone means stone that is found in nature. There are many types of stone with just as many types of color and structure.

Their firmness also varies. It extends from soft marble to hard granite. The working of stone is done by various handicrafts, but basically depends on the type of stone and the desired architectural appearance. The surfaces are cut, ground, sand-blasted, and polished.

*"Sandyline" offers flexibility and a rustic appearance*

*Natural stone, as compared to brick, does not absorb water. Thus its strengths and materials are all the more decisive.*

**Attention:** Natural stone that includes chalk, like marble, is sensitive to acids.

| **Advantages** | high pressure-resistance |
| --- | --- |
| | holds heat well |
| | can be built up quickly |
| | fire-resistant |
| | safe from rot and decay |
| | resistant to harmful organisms |
| | natural material |
| | great choice of colors |
| | wear-resistant |
| | unlimited lifetime |
| | every size is possible |
| | optically pleasing |
| **Disadvantages** | high initial cost |
| | heavy |
| | feels cool |
| | usually does not breathe actively |

### "Stoana"

Shelf forms similar to those of brick can also be made of natural stone. The stone can be used for both the load-bearing parts and the shelves. A wine shelf of natural stone looks noble and lasts forever.

But it is also more expensive than other shelves. Especially large plates for full-length shelves are more expensive and harder to obtain.

The use of these materials is especially justified in regions where a particular natural stone occurs—such as Stainz plates in western Styria.

The stones can be cut or used in rough form. In the first case, the shelves appear simple and severe. Exact shelf sizes can be made. If the stones are only cut, they look natural and original. Their use with irregular components is, of course, more difficult and expensive. The shelves are necessarily more irregular as well.

With this material the chalk content of the joints is especially important for the room climate of the wine cellar. But its disinfectant effect should also not be neglected.

### "Almost Naturally Pure"

Stone can also be combined well and effectively with other materials. If the load-bearing parts are made of natural stone, the shelves can be made, for example, of wood, glass or readymade clay pieces, such as are used as window crowns.

The combination of rough side pieces and exactly finished shelves is especially effective.

The reduced use of natural stone also makes the shelves less costly.

### "Fixed and Finished Natural Stone"

Finished systems made of natural stone can easily be combined to form high, stable shelves and can be had in the most varied shapes and sizes. There are usually special parts, such as wrought iron or glass doors, wine boxes for special bottles, dividers, and many others. DURISOL is one of the most useful systems with readymade components of building stone. The basic material is a natural building material of mineral-bound laminated wood. The porous structure, open to diffusion, affords a rustic appearance, is light, stable, and moisture-resistant, and thus offers ideal prerequisites for the proper storage of wine. There is also the option—and thus also the possibility of individual formation of one's own wine shelves—of installing single and double bottle holders, label protectors, labeling frames, and door elements.

*Natural stone complemented with massive wooden shelves*

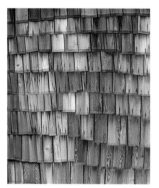

# Examples Made of Wood

## Materials and Characteristics

Wood is one of the oldest known building materials and is not inferior to other materials in durability and utility. If all aspects, such as constructive wood protection, drying, and storing are considered, wood is a long-lasting, almost unlimitedly preservable material. Wood has outstanding warmth-insulating qualities. This is important because with high room humidity no condensation occurs on the structures. Thus, dripping water cannot damage the wine bottles. Wood absorbs large amounts of excess moisture and gives them off to the environment slowly. Thus, it helps to control the climate.

Wood is a naturally growing building material and is completely removable and recyclable.

One differentiates between softwoods, such as spruce, fir, and poplar, and hardwoods like oak or beech. In between are maple, larch, alder, and ash.

Mistakes in preparing and using wood can strongly decrease its value. It is important to protect wood from various influences. Good drying protects it from fungi and insects.

To avoid odors, no paint should be used.

| | |
|---|---|
| **Advantages** | high pressure and bending resistance |
| | light material |
| | dry constructing |
| | fast constructing |
| | easy to work, mount, change |
| | corrosion-resistant |
| | favorable construction costs |
| | native material |
| | raw material keeps growing |
| | pleasant room climate |
| | pleasant natural color |
| **Disadvantages** | shrinking and expansion (movement of material) |
| | sensitivity to dampness |
| | endangered by fungi when damp |

Whoever builds his own wine cellar economically out of massive wood should definitely make sure it is stable.

The classic cellar consists of wooden planks or boards, is glued with water-insoluble glue, and also screwed (hidden).

### "All Over the Place"

This simple wooden wine shelf is decorative and nicely formed. It charms through its uniform choice of material and the symmetry of the individual sections. The angled setup, though, also causes a bit of tension in the structure.

The cabinet consists of square cubicles lying beside and above each other, with their horizontal situation tipped by 45 degrees. (Sketch 1)

The materials used are wood and wood products. The choice depends on factors of the design, the stacking height, the number of bottles, and thus their weight, but also on the desired strength of the material.

The bottles can be stacked well here, and remain—even if the cubicle is only partly filled—in their original position. The position of the individual squares depends on the number of bottles to be stored. If four bottles of a wine are purchased, the cubicles can be larger and offer space for 12 to 18 bottles. If one buys at most six bottles of a type, the cubicles can either be made smaller in general or divided by dividers.

*Thanks to the angled form, the bottles are always stable.*

These shelves can also be installed in no longer used doorways or walled-up window niches.

*Simply beautiful— beautifully simple, at Cobenzl (left), a castle on the Iron Road (right).*

For the sake of uniformity, wood can also be used for the dividers. The boards can either slide into the cubicles when needed, or be fixed in place. In the first case, the size of the cubicle can be flexibly suited to the contents. In the second, one can attain a uniform appearance of the grid, if both the dividing walls of the cubicles and the dividers are made of equally strong wood. But, one must make sure that the material strength is not too great for small cubicles, and that the division still leaves areas large enough to hold large quantities of wine. (Sketch 2)

If the cubicles are big enough or the dividers shorter than the sides, then a single bottle can be put in for decoration.

These shelf variants can be built uniformly from floor to ceiling. The top can be finished with a board, or the squares can end with points. This depends on the effect that one would like to create—closed-off or open. Also decisive, though, is the formation of the cellar ceiling, whether an arch is present or not. Whoever wants to can also combine the shelves with another variant, perhaps a horizontal one, or just create individual elements.

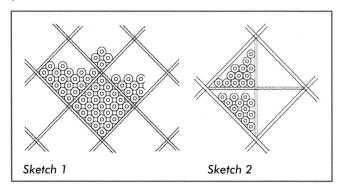

Sketch 1                    Sketch 2

### "Box"

Cubicles for 6 or 12 bottles are ideal, thus in the size order of the cartons.

These shelves are simple and lovely in their form and design. They consist of horizontal and vertical wooden boards that are united to form squares or rectangles.

They play a role both visually and constructively, depending on whether the vertical risers or horizontal shelves run the whole distance. (Sketches 1 and 2)

Solid wood is a suitable material. But it must be made in a size that will not bend under the load. In addition, single- and multiple-layered plates and other wooden materials are suitable for these shelves. They are usually more stable.

The size of the individual elements is based mainly on the number of wine bottles that one wants them to hold. One should also consider how many bottles of one type one usually buys. Naturally, one can also build larger or smaller cubicles, for static and other reasons.

*Rustic: Country house cellar in Graz (top left)*

To house special single bottles or magnums, it is also possible to make the dividers so small that just one bottle has room inside. This is, of course, somewhat laborious to build and requires precise work, but affords an optically impressive pattern and can be a thoroughly worthwhile expenditure for special wines. Thus the shelves tend a bit toward the higher ideal or material value than the bottles housed in it may have.

*Functional: Styrian Vinothek, St. Anna/Aigen (top right)*

*Classy: Lachner-Tinnacher, Steinbach (lower left)*

*Styling elements: Neumeister, Straden (lower right)*

You might put labels on the bottles or record their position (such as Cubicle C3) in a cellar book, so that you need not pull other bottles out while searching.

*Safe from slipping: angled wave principle*

*Exclusive {solitary confinement" (left)*

*Flexible cubicle division for large and small quantities of wine (right)*

In addition, they are better off protected from light than in large cubicles.

In any case, the shelves should be made stable and steady, since a filled wine shelf can hold a heavy weight. A 7/10-liter bottle weighs about 1.3 kilograms.

If one wants to divide his wine shelves into smaller units, one can do so either parallel or diagonally to the existing shelves. Both the appearance and the numbers of housed bottles are always different and must therefore be considered. In both varieties boards can simply be used once again as dividers. (Sketch 3)

In this system too, one can plan on a place for an individual bottle in each cubicle, in order to see at once what is in it.

Whoever wants his bottles to lie very securely can cut out square angled boards and attach them to the cubicle bottom. Then every bottle in the lowest row has its fixed place and cannot slip if only a few other bottles are present.

In a small space, such as behind a door, the bottles in this shelf type can also be kept standing on a narrow shelf.

## Variations

A set of shelves with a similar effect can also be built of individual elements. Here U-shaped cubicles

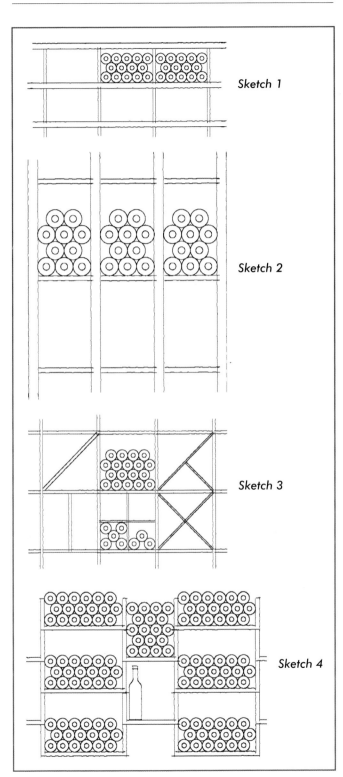

Sketch 1

Sketch 2

Sketch 3

Sketch 4

*Standing storage: a clear view but poor storage potential*

*Practical: storage in original wooden crates*

*Massive wood with metal fittings*

*A wine tower at Mitteregg; Pichler-Schober*

are built and stacked atop each other. (Sketch 4) The cubicles can be of different sizes and be designed for lying and single standing bottles. They are attached together with pegs, metal pins or angle irons. The special feature of this type is that it can be expanded at will as a kind of homemade modular system.

In this system, not only straight and symmetrical shelves can be built. Hexagonal or other multi-angled cubicles are also possible. One should just consider whether they are worth the effort.

## "Squaring the Circle"

Four equally large pieces of wood are combined here into a cube. The result is a chest without bottom or top—a frame, not for a nice picture, but for nice wine.

It is important to consider well how many bottles should have a place in the cubicle, for the lateral length of the cube is based on that. In an ideal case, one type of wine would be stored in one cube. (Sketch 1) But if one collects many different kinds of wine, and never enough of one to fill a whole cubicle, then this system with a big grid proves to be problematic and probably unsuitable. Even if one keeps order and knows where the desired bottle is lying, one must move other bottles to get to it.

In the simplest case, the individual cubes can be stacked up and attached at 90-degree angles. But it is also possible to build them up at an angle or attach them together with hardware. The latter is surely the most elaborate, but perhaps the best-looking variant.

The individual boxes are then stacked on and beside each other and attached with metal pegs or other good-looking fittings. It is important that the boxes do not stand directly on the floor, but get air. There should also be a gap between the individual boxes; otherwise the effect will be lost.

Whoever wants to achieve order and symmetry can also stack the bottles on top of each other. But that only works when the boxes have scarcely any play, being carefully measured and assembled, and then only as long as a complete row is in the cubicle. As soon as one bottle is removed, the oth-

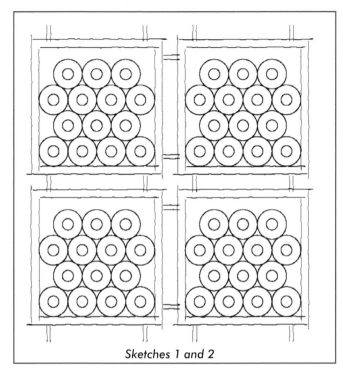

*Sketches 1 and 2*

*Custom-built: Fruehwirt Kloech*

ers slip into the spaces in the row below and the order in the system is lost! (Sketch 2)

This shelving system is ideal for growing collections. It can be expanded and built onto easily.

In combination with doors, existing bottoms can be somewhat shorter, so the door will close snugly with the box.

## "Sleeping Beauty"

No matter what one likes better—a straight or an angled wooden set of shelves—this system can be used for both: It resembles a trellis or grid. The wooden boards of the sidepieces end in angled pieces of wood. It looks light, is simple in its design, more reasonably priced, and can quickly be made at home.

*Angled wood design to be homemade.*

In the variant that runs parallel to the floor, horizontal and vertical angled pieces are screwed together alternatingly. The material strength is rather like that of a lattice. (Sketches 1, 2 and 3, page 88) With a little cutting, braces can be attached to strengthen the construction and stiffen the corners.

Dividing the cubicles into smaller units can also be done in the same system.

To prevent the wine bottles from falling off to the rear, or for optical reasons, a back wall of the shelves can be made of these angled pieces by attaching them to the sides. This resembles a so-called space board or pegboard, such as is used in simple business buildings.

In this system—as already noted—a diagonal shelf form is also possible. The principle is the same; the pieces are simply attached diagonally.

### Variations

This system can also be worked out with a few angled pieced. As a rule, two vertical pieces serve as standards, while two horizontal pieces carry the wine bottles and short cross braces serve to stiffen and connect the two frames. The wooden elements on three levels are then screwed together. (Sketches 4, 5, and 6)

*Simple construction (left), elaborate special effect (right)*

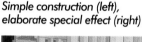

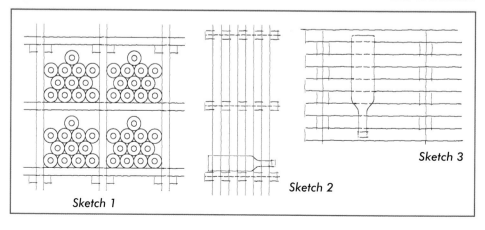

*Sketch 1*

*Sketch 2*

*Sketch 3*

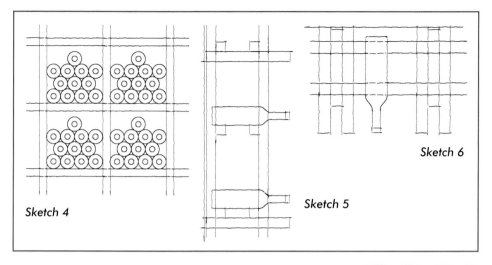

Sketch 4

Sketch 5

Sketch 6

## "Wine Party Lying Down"

The wine bottles lie in one line on this shelf. This variation is despite, or perhaps because of, its high consumption of material, one of the most striking and elegant. It is perhaps rather expensive for large stocks of wine, but quite suitable for smaller collections. (Sketch 1)

It is important to make sure that the boards are mounted exactly parallel. Any minor unevenness is noticed here immediately. (Sketch 2)

This shelf can be fitted into a wall niche. If this does not work, one must—to prevent the bottles from rolling out sideways—attach a vertical board. But this should be thin, so as not to destroy the fineness and special effect of the design. (Sketch 3)

In this example the choice of suitable wood is especially important, for in thick wooden boards the color and veining are decisive.

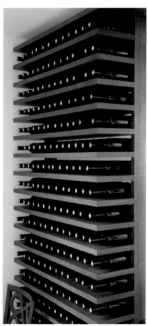

*Style element: Frühwirt*

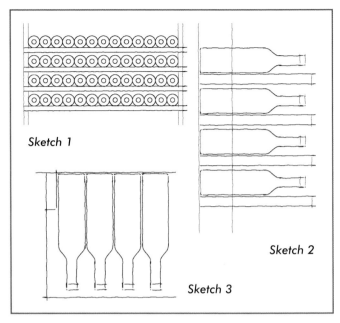

Sketch 1

Sketch 2

Sketch 3

## "Stiltwalking"

These shelves are made by combining individual modules and screwing them together. Thus it is easy to expand. If necessary, one simply stacks the modules up.

The module consists of wood, which is sawed raw in the simplest case, but can also be planed.

One element consists of three boards. Two form the load-bearing frame, one the bottom. The height of the sidepieces is based on the desired stacking height, the length of the bottom shelf on how many bottles are to find room on it in one line. The individual modules are screwed together with wooden slats. They should prevent the shelves from tipping sideways, guarantee secure standing even with great stacking heights, and naturally carry the shelf with the wine bottles. Even under the last element, two slats can be attached. They strengthen the structure. (Sketches 1 and 2)

If a module is added later—to an already well-filled wine shelf—it is practical to attach the slats to the sides of the already existing shelves and then lay the new shelf on top of them. Naturally, the shelves can grow not only vertically but also horizontally.

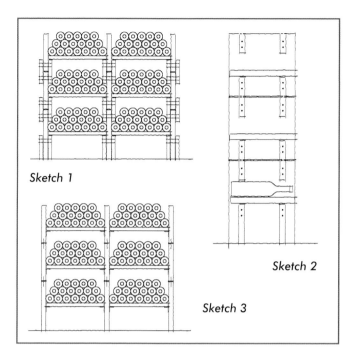

Sketch 1

Sketch 2

Sketch 3

If the structure with slats is too crude for you, you can also attach the side pieces over each other with metal pins. The shelves can be mounted on angle irons. (Sketch 3)

## "Gaunta"

This is surely one of the simplest variants. The shelf consists exclusively of wood. No great demands are made on the material in terms of veining and surface treatment. It is simple in design and construction. Its nature reminds one a bit of the simple four-cornered wooden beams on which the big barrels and small barriques are stored in wine cellars. These] structures are called "Gaunta" in the Styrian dialect, and called "Ganter" in the talk of the trade.

The shelves consist of full-length horizontal and interrupted vertical wooden boards. The latter can be joined to form a grid of angled pieces attached under the shelf bottom by angle irons or screwed or nailed into the corners. (Sketch) Over the shelf bottom, halved posts hold the upright boards or shelf uprights. These three-cornered pieces not only provide stiffness and thus stability to the shelves, but also separate the structure. Thus various types and vintages can be housed simply and visibly. It is important to bring the simple wooden shelves out of the possibly damper and cooler bottom area. This is simple to do by placing the first board, for example, on a tarred railroad tie or a simple brick foundation.

*Wooden barrels are traditionally stored on "Gantern."*

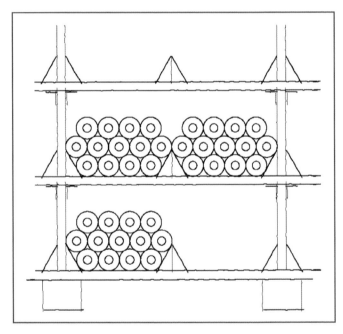

## "Everything in Frames"

Here is another very simple way to build wine shelves. The advantage is that only one material is used and the structure is easy to assemble. It can be fitted easily to uneven floors and does not cost much to build.

It consists of vertical carrier elements made of wood. If real wood is used, the cross-sections can be nearly square. Such standards are called posts. But it is also possible to use boards as uprights. Either wooden boards that, if need be, can be screwed together of two or three pieces and thus strengthened, for example, because of the heavy weight of the bottles, or standards in board form made of laminated plates. The latter are more stable because they are glued together. (Sketch 1)

When uprights of wood are used, it is important that no rising moisture is present. With slightly damp floors, metal risers or plastic underlay can help.

Simple wooden boards are then attached to these wooden uprights. They can be screwed or attached with angle irons. It is important that both the board and the connector can bear the weight of the bottles. (Sketch 2)

The bottle lies with its neck on the front frame. So that this works out in practice, the two wooden boards—if they are equally wide—must be mounted at different heights. In any case, the bottle should lie evenly on the finished shelf!

WHEN clay soil is NOT suitable!

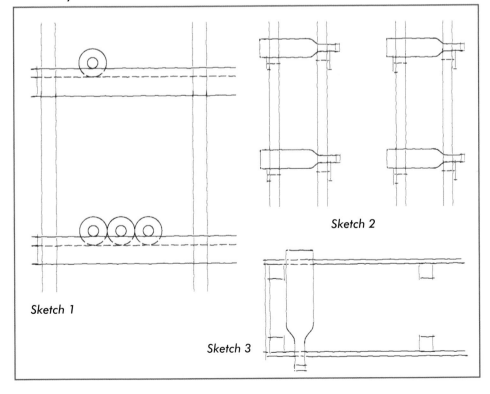

Sketch 1

Sketch 2

Sketch 3

It is also important that the rear gap between the shelves and the wall is not too great; otherwise there may be a danger of bottles falling off.

The distance of the uprights to each other results naturally from static reasons. But the uprights also divide the shelf bottoms into individual cubicles. Thus, the bottles are prevented in the simplest way from rolling into another cubicle. (Sketch 3)

To prevent the shelves from tipping, or even falling, mounting a brace or stiffener is necessary. For this, either metal rods in X-form or, in the simplest case, laths nailed to the back of the shelves, will do. Sometimes it can be practical to attach the shelves to a point on the wall as well.

### "Racks"

The wine shelves assembled under this heading are a simple rack as developed for the production of champagne.

To create this rack, one uses simple wooden boards in which holes the size of a bottleneck are drilled. The borings should be vertical to the board or steeper, so that the bottles cannot fall out. The gaps between them are more than a bottle's diameter. It is important that the board is wide enough so that enough board is still left after the holes are drilled. (Sketches 1 and 2)

These individual boards are attached to the wall and floor at regular intervals to each other, using three-cornered wooden wedges. The wooden boards should not be too high so all bottles can be

*A rack such as is used in traditional bottle fermentation; Regele, Berghausen (left); a wall design, Wellanschitz (right)*

reached easily and safely. In addition, overextended boards bend under the weight and the angle at which the bottles are inserted becomes too small. The bottles can then fall out.

Each pair of boards should be placed some distance apart, so that the empty space between the wine shelf and the wall can be cleaned, for it is always possible for bottles to break or leak.

If one puts two such boards together—like a real rack—it becomes a free-standing element in the room and can be loaded from both sides. (Sketch 3)

## VARiANT 1

It is very easy to set up a wine holder by taking an old wooden door, boring holes in it, and mounting the door on the wall at an angle.

## VARiANT 2

The boards can also be mounted at an angle by using wedges. The bottles then are stuck in to form rows parallel to the floor. To be sure, more wedges are needed, and the boards must be attached parallel to each other, but less space is needed, since the shelves do not extend so far into the cellar area. (Sketches 4 and 5)

The boards do not have to be attached like a kind of inverted sheathing. There can also be vertical angled strips of wood attached to the wall. Boards are then screwed to them as intervals. It looks nice when the interval of the boards to each

HERE bACkGROUNd liGHTiNG CAN bE VERY EFFECTiVE.

*The conical borehole allows different angles and different-sized bottles*

*A hint of tradition: Racks and wooden cases: Gols*

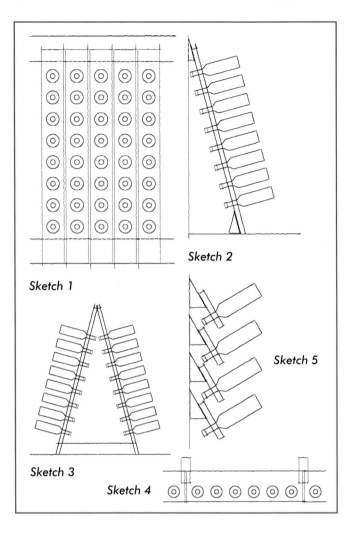

Sketch 1

Sketch 2

Sketch 3

Sketch 4

Sketch 5

other more or less corresponds to their thickness. (Sketches 6 and 7)

One can also fasten several boards together to form a square. One simply leaves more space to the other boards. (Sketch 8)

If individual boards are made of different kinds of wood or painted different colors, one not only achieves a nice effect, but can also arrange the stored wines clearly by type.

### Variant 3

This system is harder to build, but perhaps more impressive. Walls that do not look good, or

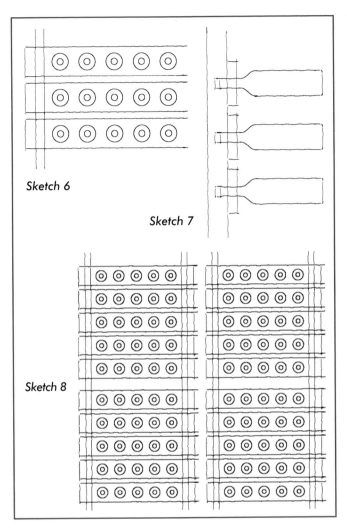

Sketch 6

Sketch 7

Sketch 8

brickwork that should breathe and thus remain un-plastered, can be hidden behind a wooden wall that one can use simultaneously as a wine shelf. The wall can consist of boards or laminated wood.

## Variant 4

By using this bored-hole system, one can also set up two wooden walls at a distance from each other. It is important, as with all shelves, that they be stable and will not break under the weight of the bottles.

One bores holes the size of the bottle diameter in the first wooden panel, and holes the diameter

If individual bottles are placed on the shelf standing, they make viewing them easier, for they indicate the contents of the shelf.

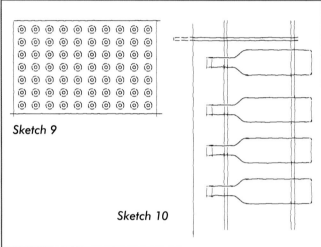

*Sketch 9*

*Sketch 10*

of the bottleneck in the second one. One must, of course, be sure that the center of the holes' diameters are exactly over each other; otherwise the bottles will not lie exactly, horizontally on the rack. (Sketches 9 and 10)

## "Always Around and Around"

WHOEVER WANTS TO CAN ALSO PAINT THE REAR WALL AS A SEALER, OR CAN MAKE IT OF, FOR EXAMPLE, SHEET METAL OR GLASS.

Here is one way to store wine individually. A transparent wooden grid holds the bottles. The shelf is especially elegant and effective when the components are made delicate and thin.

In small form, it is suitable for only a few bottles, but it can also be expanded as high shelves. (Sketches 1 and 2)

Several bottles can also be stored in one cubicle. One simply increases the vertical interval of the uprights and the horizontal intervals of the standards. One places a board bottom on it to hold the bottles. (Sketch 3)

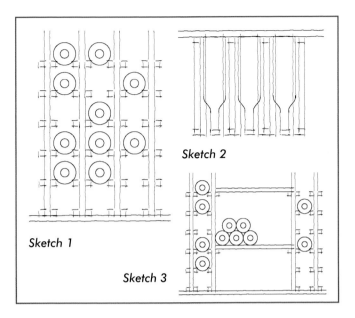

Sketch 1

Sketch 2

Sketch 3

*A nice combination of wood and glass; Umathum*

This system can be built with a rear wall of wood or some other material.

This shelf variant also has its charm without a rear wall. Background lighting makes a striking impression of the bottles.

## "Head or Number"

A row of bottles covers the wall. All the wines are visible at first glance, and the labels—if turned the right way—are easy to read.

Whoever likes to have his collection visible and preserve a good view of it will find this variant right for him. But it is also suitable for narrower cellar spaces and niches, for large bottles, and even for storage in the kitchen until the wines are drunk.

The system is the same as with the wooden crates in which one buys the wine.

The bottles are placed horizontally in a rack on the wall. This carrier construction can be made of wooden or laminated boards. The boards must be wider than one bottle diameter. Holes are bored for them in the sizes of the bottle diameters and necks. Even the borehole in which the whole bottle fits must have enough play. (Sketch 3)

These wooden boards are attached by angle irons to the wall vertically at the thin side. The interval must be chosen so that the bottle does not slide out. To store a bottle, one needs a small borehole to hold the neck and a large one for the whole diameter of the bottle. It is important that the midpoints of the holes be exactly over each other. (Sketches 1 and 2)

One can arrange all the bottles in the same direction or alternate them. (Sketch 4)

### VARiANT

If the wooden structure seems too weighty, then metal angle irons can also be used as brackets. They are naturally harder to bore holes for, but more delicate in their structure, and they show more of the bottle and its label. The latter, to be sure, can also be damaged more easily by improper storage and the use of metal. (Sketch 5)

*St. Urban, patron saint of wine*

If one wants to place several of these wine-bottle racks side by side, one must not only make sure that the boards are really mounted parallel to each other, but especially that there is enough lateral space to the next wine bottle and thus space to remove it.

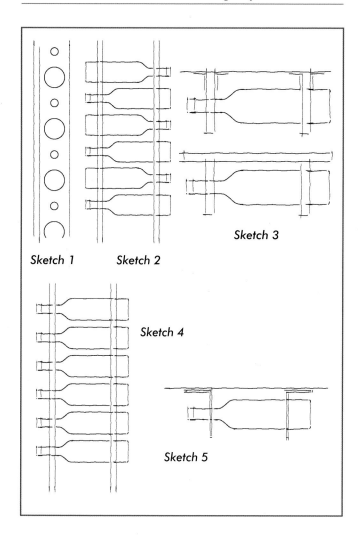

Sketch 1 Sketch 2 Sketch 3

Sketch 4

Sketch 5

## "On the Wall, On the Wall..."

Wine is stored here on simple wooden boards. They are somewhat wider than the diameter of a bottle and are screwed to the wall horizontally like ordinary shelves. The bottles lie on them one after another, like the cars of a train.

It is only important that the bottles do not roll off the shelf. To prevent that, one can attach the board tilted slightly to the back or attach a lath to the front edge. More elegant in their workmanship and appearance, though, are the types in which the board is somewhat reamed out. It can be angular or rounded—fitting the roundness of the bottle.

HERE AND THERE EQUALLY wide vertical boards support the structure and thus form a frame for the individual wine types.

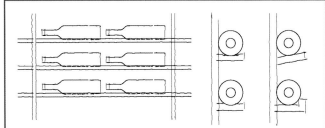

*Large-scale
in terms of surface...*

*... space-saving
in terms of depth! Rauch*

WHEN CHOOSING THE
MATERIAL, MAKE SURE THAT
STABILITY AND PERMANENCE
WILL BE PROVIDED, ESPECIALLY
IN CASE DAMPNESS OCCURS
DURING STORAGE.

## "Fixed and Finished Wood"

In this realm, the choice of shelf systems is gigantic. Almost all shelves—even if they are not meant primarily for wine storage—can be adapted suitably and, optically as well as functionally, result in a unique, individual wine shelf. Perhaps in a builders' market, one or another furniture store, or on the Internet, you will find a set of shelves that can be adapted into a suitable wine shelf. Sometimes separate elements can be quickly and functionally combined. (Sketch)

Several wines can be stored in the larger cubicles. If the individual parts are mounted one above the other by means of spacers like a wood block or a brick, the result can be a small cabinet for individual bottles or a larger one for wine in cartons.

In Switzerland CAVEAU STAR has specialized in the production of wooden structures for both bottle and box storage. Under the motto "The perfect bottle cabinet for your wine cellar," they work from a basic model to offer individual solutions. In the components of the system, they stress perfect type and vintage separation of wines, plus a space-saving and visually impressive view of the wine shelf. Planning and production are offered on an individual basis working from an assortment with twenty models.

The shelves are built of practically branch-free fir wood that is planed on all sides and etched in an immersion process (water-etching). The shelves offer safe and sure storage, plus space for 2 to 24 bottles. In planning your shelves, especially the cubicle sizes, you should remember that bottles come in various shapes and that not every means of storage is suitable for all types of bottles. The basic structures are all 200 cm high and are available

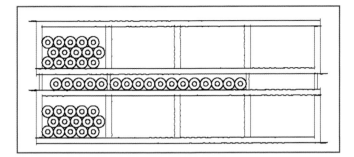

with 32 cm depth (51 cm for wooden crates) and varying widths from 55 to 109 cm. Depending on the model, they offer space for 128 to 250 bottles or at least eight crates or cartons in the version with full tables, which can result in easier removal of bottles, even when fully loaded.

Les Casiers d'Antan, a French producer of wine furniture and accessories, traditionally sticks to solid French oak with linseed-oil coating. Not only for the wine, but also for the bottle storage, great firmness and aging conditions are stressed, and the wine shelf becomes a piece of furniture that suits the highest requirements and thus goes well not only in dark cellars but also in dwelling and selling areas, restaurants, and vinotheks (wine libraries— specialty wine shops educating customers about local wines). The standard shelves are designed for 12 to 168 bottles and suitable for all current bottle types, including magnums, thanks to special cutouts

*Individual formative possibilities*

in the shelf carriers. The same shelves are suitable for various upper structures: leaning storage for presentation and selling purposes or flat storage. Tilted presentation surfaces can be combined with flat types as one wishes. The shelves themselves can be expanded with several accessories. Thus one shelf cover, which is offered in three sizes, offers a nice finish and at once allows the placing of individual bottles, cartons or wooden crates. If the storage cellar is also used as a tasting room, empty bottles of high-priced wines—of which one has fond memories—can be placed on the shelf. For the storage of wine in wooden boxes, so-called crate insertion modules, which can be assembled in many variants, are available. For better visibility, these crate shelves can be enclosed with glass panels, so that the crate shelf can also serve as a place to put glasses. To be able to find the wines again, it is vital not only to sort them, but also to mark them. For this purpose, and to lend an air of value and elegance, one's own label holders of polished brass are foreseen. The complete assortment is just as suitable for the private wine lover as for the professional.

ROBBY-BOX Click-Stick Systems of the German manufacturer Drehvo GmbH are sold exclusively through the wine trade and constitute a very light and flexible system. One shelf element is laid out for the horizontal storage of six bottles. The shelf elements, made of 8-mm laminated birch

In case all the bottles on one shelf are to be presented tilted, this decreases the capacity of the shelves by half!

*Practical storage in original wooden crates on sliding shelf elements*

wood (measuring 450 x 300 x 110 mm) that can be stacked very simply to a height of 2.6 meters, are very stable and long-lived. With appropriate connecting elements, compatibility and additional stability are provided side by side, and for the observer it is really a very impressive view. The load strength is stated as having a maximum stacking pressure of 950 kilograms.

*Lovely form with 12 in a row*

The unfinished birch laminate can very easily be finished for optical matching with the corresponding colored finish in nature, light oak, teak, dark green, dark red or mahogany. Whoever would rather store his wines in wooden crates but not spend the money for the wines that are traditionally packed that way has the frame with the wine box for 6 or 12 bottles and then need only add the desired contents. Possibly used by the vintner as a shipping crate, this serves you immediately for the proper storage of your wines. The combi-box has an already stamped front side that opens by simply pressing on the lid; then it can be used simply as a stacking box. The boxes can be stacked up to 2.6 meters, are extremely stable and long-lived. They have a load-bearing capacity of 40 kilograms and hold a stacking pressure of 950 kg. The length (400 mm) and width (270 mm) is the same for 6- or 12-bottle boxes; the height varies from 190 mm (6) to 340 mm (12). Each wine box has an opening on the front for easy removal of the wine. For good visibility, bottle holders that can be mounted very easily on the fronts of the boxes are recommended.

*Single-bottle holder by Robby Box*

*Transport and storage elements in a row*

The MS-380 wine shelf made by Mueller-Soppart is a solid, reasonably priced design made of native conifer woods that have been treated with preservatives. The cubicles are designed for twelve bottles and, with a depth of 43 cm and a storage capacity of some 170 bottles, per square meter, are also space saving.

The MS-700 variant, unlike the MS-380, has larger-sized laths with rounded edges. The surface is polished and painted, which improves the appearance and thus changes the shelves from a subdued storage system into a piece of furniture. The cubicle size is laid out for 18 to 35 bottles—depending on the type of stacking—and measures 33 x 41 x 47 cm

*Stackable storage elements in a row*

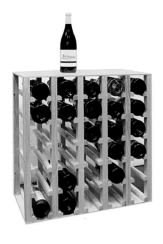

in height, width, and depth. Each cubicle can also be fitted with an inserted diagonal board or a crossbar, so that up to four very small cubicles result, which again heightens the flexibility for single bottles and special formats and also relaxes the appearance. The compact model has a storage capacity of more than 210 bottles per square meter of wall space.

The MS-735 Gand-Cru model is offered especially for storing wooden crates. For this, slide rails are installed in the cubicles, so that every crate can be pulled out up to 4/5 of its length to make taking bottles out easier. The cubicles measure 25 cm high, 33.5 cm wide, and 52 cm deep, and offer space for one wooden crate or 21 Bordeaux bottles, stacked shoulder to shoulder.

The MS-STAPELKISTE (MS-STACK BOX) can be built up in high or diagonal format to form a big wine-cellar wall of shelves. The rear wall of the stacked box is made of plywood, the sides of 2-cm solid wood. With a storage capacity of 15 bottles and dimensions of 43 x 30 x 33.5 (height/width/depth), it has a storage capacity of about 116 bottles per square meter. Not much stands in the way of your imagination when you assemble your own wall of shelves! The stacking crates are stable enough to be mounted on the wall with appropriate attachments. Offset half a cubicle width, they form a decorative wall shelf unit that is thoroughly suitable for homes and salesrooms. And with the use of bottle holders besides the crates, a good view is afforded.

*Simple and practical solutions*

Well suited to storing individual bottles is the MS-SINGLE system, in which the bottles lie on just two points (compared to the "always around" system). The standard shelves are offered with a capacity of up to 30 bottles and dimensions of 62 x 60 x 30 cm, which provides for 80 bottles per square meter. The standard elements are again individually stackable, with the stability additionally increased by offset stacking. The MS-Single shelves are also available as the MS-SINGLE MAGNUM for magnum bottles. Elegant appearance, large-scale simplicity, and absolute holding of the bottles characterize the system.

All MS shelves are delivered assembled, so that only the horizontal laths need to be screwed on.

## "Wintower"

Based on a small number of standard components, an attempt is made to offer as many combinations as possible. Vertical elements at lengths of 96, 139, and 192 cm are offered with rail operation on one or both sides, horizontal parts 33 cm deep can be had in five different widths for bottles and magnums, with surface dimensions given in parentheses:

- for one bottle (70-84 mm)

- for 1 magnum of champagne (84-108 mm)

- for 3 bottles (70-84 mm)

- for 4 bottles (70-84 mm) or 3 magnums (84-108 mm)

- for 6 bottles (70-84 mm) or 4 magnums (84-121 mm)

*Modular principle with simple wooden crates*

With a depth of 53 cm, there is only shelf room for 3, 4, and 6 bottles.

The system itself functions by a rail principle. Shelf bottoms can be slid between sidepieces of various heights. Through small offsets of the rails, the change of the cubicle height can be made in 2-cm steps. A decisive advantage over other systems is that neither tools nor screws are needed. The stability of the whole shelf unit is based on the construction of the rail and drawer elements. All the components are deliberately made of wood, so that it is suitable, has esthetic qualities, offers the most varied possibilities, and also shares warmth and yet is stable. The panels are watertight and show appropriate stability despite high air humidity. The Belgian manufacturer Lecellier spri offers individual planning and combinations of its personal shelves. Depending on available space and bottles to be stored, any combination can be planned for and calculated in advance. If the foundation on which the shelves are to stand shows heavy moisture, it is recommended either to place the shelves on the available plastic base or avoid direct absorption of water with bricks or screw feet under the panels.

*High flexibility and stability through variable cubicle sizes*

*The Masterpiece*

*The steel bottle racks are decorative and elegant*

### "Your Carpenter Makes It Personally"

Along with the shelves designed and built by us and the finished systems available in the trade, there is also a variety of other possibilities and solutions. If you have a good idea or a solid concept of how your wine shelves should look, you can also have it built by your carpenter. But even without a firm concept of your own, your carpenter can surely help; for example, Master Carpenter Michael Altenbacher created his "In vino veritas" wine shelf unit. His idea was to design a piece of furniture that could stand freely in the room as a sculpture and fulfill a function. A harmonious blend of wood, metal, and glass was to be attained. The flowing form of the shelf is to be brought into harmony with the bodies. The waved elements of walnut and stainless steel are copied from nature (grapevines, waterfalls). The bodies were made of solid field maple and reinforced on the corners. It is all meant to look as if it were a single casting.

## Examples Made of Wood and Metal

### "Steinbach 12"

In this shelf system, the load-bearing parts are made of rectangular metal standards. Naturally, the use of metal pipes would also have been possible. Here, though, the forming of connections to the shelves proves to be more difficult, since the contact surfaces are not at right angles. The use of metal, as compared to wood, allows smaller cross-sections. The shelves thus appear lighter and more elegant.

Since cellar floors and ceilings are often very uneven, it makes sense to make the standards in the shelf area and the connections to the ceiling height-adjustable (by means of screws) and elastic (equalizing buffers).

The actual cubicles that hold the wine bottles are U-shaped wooden pieces that are attached to the standards by angle irons or metal pins.

---

**With shelves that impress by their symmetry and straight lines, it is especially important that the bottles do not have too much play on the shelf. Otherwise they may slip back and forth, and the bottles in the second row will not lie exactly at one level. This is especially noticeable in such uniform shelves.**

---

One criterion in the manufacture is the lateral height of the shelves. If they are too low, the bottles are not held. But if they are too high, the shelves lose the lightness of their design. For it is the fine, delicate structure that makes it simple and elegant. Naturally, the distance of the shelves from the floor and ceiling also contributes to the effect. (Sketch)

The shelves stand directly at the wall, without rear ventilation. This is possible in dry cellars and shelf systems that are not thoroughly filled with bottles to their full height. Despite this, the wall can breathe. In this variant, it is then not necessary to extend all the standards from the floor to the ceiling.

Here, for example, only the front standards are stretched between the floor and ceiling. The back ones are attached directly to the wall. This structure appears light and elegant, but it also gives the shelves more stability, which is especially important for long, high wine shelves that must carry great weight.

*The successful contrast of functionality and design: Lackner-Tinnacher*

### Variant 1

Whoever wants to can also make the shelf widths vary, so as to house different quantities of bottles. A height variation is also possible. But here the shelves lose their charm and unity.

### Variant 2

It is also possible to mount only boards instead of the U-shaped drawers. One must make sure that the bottles cannot roll from one drawer into another.

### Variant 3

The standards can naturally also be made of wood. The thicknesses will then be correspondingly larger.

The shelves are also a good example for growing collections. Here one can build and install only a part of the shelves at the first stage. They can be expanded in both height and width. In the first variant, the extension consists of additional standards and drawers, in the latter, only additional drawers are mounted when needed.

*Stacked bottles with a decorative effect, at Polz, Spielfeld*

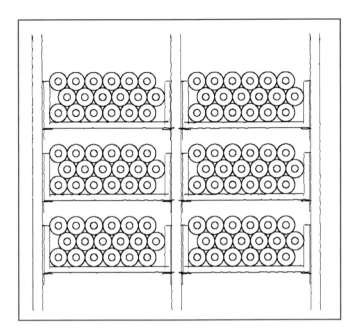

## "A Bird on the Wire"

In this variation, a wide wooden frame or wide wooden upright is combined with a delicate horizontal metal structure. (Sketch 2) The wood forms the actual supporting structure. The wine bottles always lie on two metal rods, both of which ideally extend in one piece through the entire shelf structure and are regularly supported by vertical wooden pieces in between.

It is recommended that the length and width between the carrying wooden frame members be based on a certain number of bottles.

One criterion in construction is also the length of the metal rods. It is important that the rods can be fitted into the structure, even in a long shelf unit. If that is not possible, then separate short metal rods must be used. Then one must make sure that the rods have enough carrying surface in the wooden structure. Depending on the width of the wooden frame and the number of bars, the bottles cannot only be housed in series, one after another, but also lie parallel to each other in the depth. (Sketches 1 and 3)

This shelf unit looks light, transparent, shows off the bottles well, and can be used either as

The parallel interval of the metal rods from each other must logically be smaller than the diameter of the wine bottles.

*A room divider of a somewhat different kind in San Pietro, Graz*

shelves against a wall or as a room divider. As a separating element it can be made very slim and delicate, or deeper, since wines can be reached from both sides.

For safety's sake, this shelf unit should be attached to either the wall, floor or ceiling.

Whoever wants to can also set up several short sliding units as in a drugstore or kitchen pantry, and combine them with each other. The bottles are then stored very much in darkness, but are moved when the unit is drawn out. This variant can also be made with a decorative wooden plate on top as a place to keep or set glasses. (Sketch 4)

These shelves also look decorative when individual bottles are kept behind clear or frosted glass. Their combination with lights is especially charming. The lights, though, should not be turned on too often or too long. And do not expose the special rarities of your wine cellar to the light!

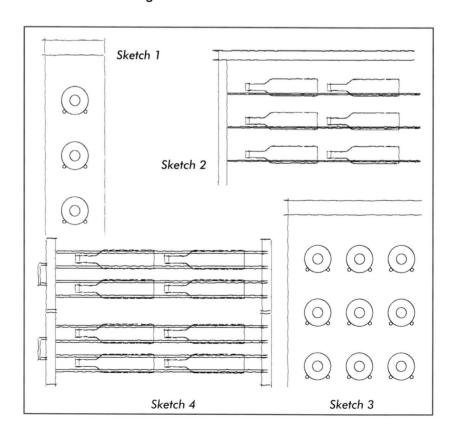

Sketch 1

Sketch 2

Sketch 4

Sketch 3

### "LK"

This shelf unit is a combination of wood and metal. According to taste and preference for materials, either the wood or the metal part can be emphasized in the structure.

If the wood is to dominate, one makes a shelf of rectangular grid elements. Metal rods are inserted in them from top to bottom through previously bored holes. The light interval of the rods equals the distance of the bottle diameter. Whoever wants to can also make some intervals larger, so as to store magnum bottles in them. It is important, though, that the holes line up exactly.

The length of the individual rods may also be only great enough so that they can be included in the design without problems. Otherwise they have to be made in pieces. (Sketches 1 and 2)

The shelf unit looks especially unified and symmetrical, since the bottles lie right over each other in their positions, and their places remain unchanged after other bottles are removed. Thus there is no sliding!

The bottles should have a little clearance from the shelf above them, so that they can be removed easily. With the resulting rows and cubicles, the wine on the shelves is very easy to see. The needed space is somewhat greater, to be sure, than in other systems, but the order is guaranteed!

If one or more cubicles are fitted with doors, then doors of glass or Plexiglas are best suited to this system. Thus the grid formed by the metal bars

*Stable storage to the last bottle, but not suitable for Burgundy or Rhine wine bottles!*

---

In the height of the individual cubicles at least six bottles—the contents of one carton—should have space.

---

*Individual cubicles with metal bars and closing doors*

remains visible; the door itself is almost invisible. Naturally, they can also be made with locks to protect especially valuable bottles.

The shelves can also be set up a few centimeters from the cellar wall. This version is recommended where there are uneven walls, walls to which attachment is very difficult or complicated, or when the surface of the wall is not to be disturbed by attachments (glass, tile, wood, etc.), when the walls are not completely dry. This separation creates an evaporation surface. This separation is also necessary when the wall material looks artistic and should attract attention (tile, natural stone, nice plaster surface, paint).

In the last case in particular, the combination with background lighting is recommended. A few centimeters are enough of a gap.

The background lighting makes not only the bottles but also the material of the wall stand out. The light source can be mounted on either the wall or, more ideally and effectively, on the floor level.

To give the shelves more stability, they must be reinforced. Since the gap to the back wall is very large here, this reinforcement must be combined with a way to prevent bottles from falling out.

Wines that are stored in wooden crates or cartons can find room in this system. One simply

BE SURE THAT THE GAP IS NOT TOO BIG AND THAT BOTTLES CANNOT FALL OUT TO THE REAR!

*A flexible storage system with maximum space utilization at Pogusch.*

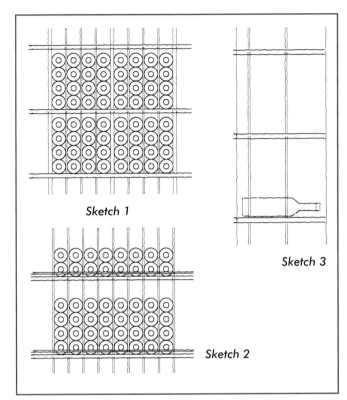

Sketch 1

Sketch 2

Sketch 3

WHOEVER WANTS TO CAN fit these shelves with a wooden cover plate. This is useful for decanting, or simply to store newly bought wine before it is sorted out.

*A metal railing with additional uses*

makes the intervals between the metal rods big enough. The holes for the 7/10 bottle grid can still be made, and the remaining rods can be inserted only when needed.

If the metal parts are to dominate this shelf type, wood is used in the form of boards, only for horizontal shelf bottoms. The metal standards form the actual shelf grid. These variants look light, transparent, and can be fitted to any type of space.

So that the bottles lie safely—which is especially important with great stacking heights—a horizontal metal rod at the height of the bottle necks can provide support. (Sketch 3)

This system is also suitable for combining with others. For example, it can be set on a brick or wooden shelf unit that is some 90 cm tall (working height).

If that is not the case, the bottles must be stored away from the floor on a type of base. One can do this with a wooden platform or a low brick foundation. The metal standards can also find a secure hold. (Sketches 4 and 5)

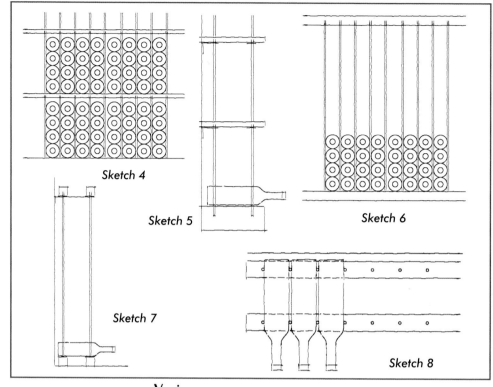

Sketch 4

Sketch 5

Sketch 6

Sketch 7

Sketch 8

## Variant

Such a shelf unit can also be assembled from pre-assembled parts. One takes two railing elements, such as those used for safety on balconies and railings, and mounts them at appropriate distances from the wall and each other. It is only important that the interval of the standards be nearly that of the bottles and the railings are securely fastened to each other and to the wall. (Sketches 6, 7 and 8)

### "Fully Released"

A possible way to build a wine shelf without supports or standards is shown here.

For it, one needs wooden boards as wide as a wine bottle is tall. The boards, of whatever material, should be that wide. Solid wooden boards are usually somewhat harder to cut to size than others, but that does not detract from the beauty of the shelves. Quite the opposite: It affords a good

*Classic attachment for shelf bottoms*

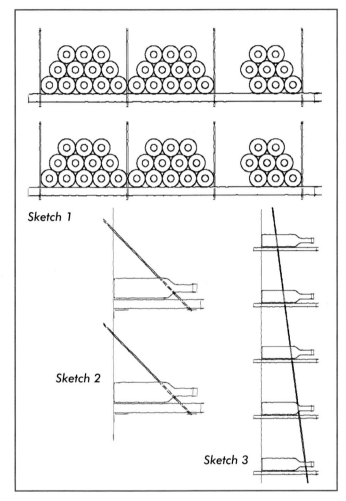

Sketch 1

Sketch 2

Sketch 3

The shelves can be mounted at right angles to the wall or with the front edge unnoticeably tilted upward. In no case should the bottles be able to slide off the shelves.

contrast to the light metal structure of the attachments. (Sketch 2)

As already noted, the boards are held by metal rods or wires. The wooden shelves are attached to the wall with angle irons. The parallel interval is based on the height of the bottle stack. To assure the wines a secure hold, the boards are bored through at the front edge and secured by being hung from the wall by steel cable, rods or frames. (Sketch 1)

## Variant

If one does not want to mount each shelf separately, one can also secure several boards with a metal rod or tube. In the area where they are attached to the wall, they are either attached with angle irons, as in the previous example, or set into the wall. A metal element running at an angle from the wall or ceiling to the floor links the shelves and also holds them firmly in place. (Sketch 3)

In both variants, the shelves are fixed and thus hard to change. The shelves themselves, though, are very handy and offer much space for wine in a simple manner.

## Examples Made of Metal

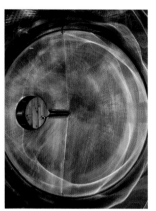

### Materials and Characteristics

Since civilization began, metals have found many uses as working materials.

They were so important that phases of human development were named after them (Bronze Age, Iron Age). They are divided into light and heavy metals according to their weight. Pure metals are almost never used. The combination of different metals with each other is called alloying. Alloys often have very different properties than the pure metals.

The most important light metal is aluminum, and the most important heavy metal is steel in its many alloy forms.

But they can also lie on metal posts.

| Advantages | Very firm against pulling |
|---|---|
| | Dry building method |
| | Withstands fire |
| | Repels rot and decay |
| | Resistant to parasites |
| | Easy to mount and change |
| | No dampness in building |
| | Enduring |
| | Small cross-section |
| **Disadvantages** | Poor warmth insulation |
| | Not always non-corroding |
| | High material costs |

## "Less is More"

Both the frame structure and the cubicles consist of metal in this version. The most varied forms can be welded together for the frame—square or rectangular elements as well as I-, T- or U-shaped types. Either only corner pieces or whole sides can form the load-bearing structure of the frame. (Sketches 1, 2 and 3)

In metal structures, though, it is especially important that they be made precisely. Uneven floors can cause problems.

The inserted bottoms of the cubicles are made of sheet metal. Here too, no boundaries to imagination are set. The bottles can be placed in the frame either horizontally or slightly tilted to the back. They can be held by straight or angled sheet-metal panels. (Sketches 4-8)

This shelf system is rather demanding and cost-intensive, but appears noble and elegant through the appropriate use of materials.

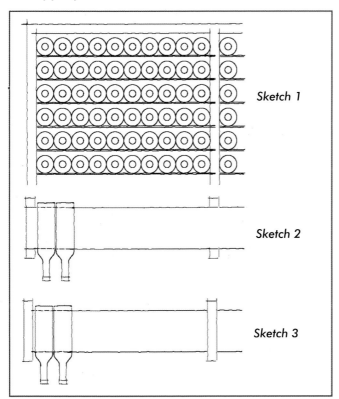

*Sketch 1*

*Sketch 2*

*Sketch 3*

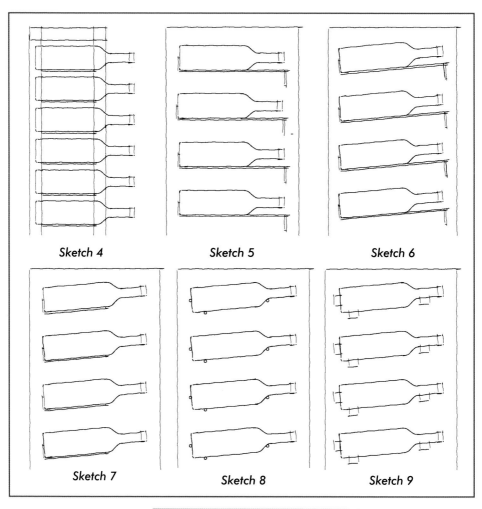

*Sketch 4*

*Sketch 5*

*Sketch 6*

*Sketch 7*

*Sketch 8*

*Sketch 9*

*Weninger Design, Horitschon*

*Stacked bottles with an inspiring effect near Fruehwirt, Kloech*

## Variant 1

Whoever finds the metal structure burdensome can make the standards or frame structure out of wood and screw the metal cubicles to them.

## Variant 2

The inserted bottoms can also be made of glass. This lends the structure a certain transparency.

## Variant 3

A good contrast is also formed by a metal frame and angled wooden strips that hold the bottles. (sketch 9)

## "12 Under Par"

This system consists of metal profiles that are attached vertically to a wall.

To create a certain lightness, it is recommended that the profiles not be mounted all the way from floor to ceiling, but to leave a gap both above and below. This wine-storage variant is especially suited for uneven floors or cellars in which the floor covering may not be burdened.

An even—at best plastered—wall surface is important. L-profiles are best for the carrying structure. But box or U-shaped profiles with flanges can also be used for mounting. Holes are bored in the profiles. (Sketches 1 and 2)

Two metal panels carry each individual bottle by the neck.

For magnum bottles, a larger gap between holes should be assured, also toward the wall!

*A very visible wall frame for storing individual bottles*

Since the holes are somewhat larger than the bottle necks, the holes in the two metal plates must be bored offset at the difference of hole diameter to bottle diameter. (Sketch 5) If that is not done, the bottles will not stay horizontal in the holes, but tip slightly downward. In the slightest case, this is just an optical fault. In the worst case, though, the bottle may even fall out.

This wine-storage system is easy to see, effective, and lets the wall surface as well as each individual bottle be seen. It can be used for entire wall surfaces as well as narrow niches or single elements, as for the storage of special wine bottles or magnum bottles. Openings in the wall can also be cut out easily, and windows are easily accessible.

All labels are easy to read without moving the bottles.

If several profiles are mounted on a wall parallel to each other, one must make sure that the bottles can be inserted and removed. For this, either the distance between profiles or the horizontal intervals of the bottles must be big enough. (Sketch 4)

This variant can also be made optionally with angled wood pieces or boards.

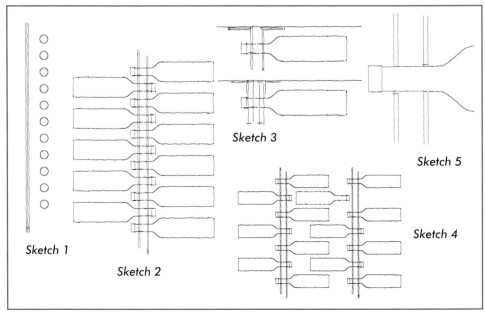

Sketch 3

Sketch 5

Sketch 4

Sketch 1

Sketch 2

## "Checkmate!"

As a simple and practical shelf variant that consists completely of metal, a steel grid, available in the trade, may be used for storage where there are concrete ceilings and walls.

This system looks light, lets a good-looking wall behind it show through, is usable at uneven walls, and allows the storage of a number of bottles on a small surface.

So that it can be used for the storage of wine bottles, an appropriate size of grid must be chosen. This depends on the diameter of the bottles. The rectangular grid should, on the one hand, not be too big, so that the bottles are not too loose. On the other hand, the grid must also not be too small to hold bottles with larger diameters (such as champagne bottles). A grid size between 8 and 10 cm is recommended. For individual larger bottle diameters, one piece of the grid can be cut out, so that four smaller rectangles become one large one. (Sketch 1)

Steel grids are available in sizes from 5 x 2.15 meters and 6 x 2.4 meters. They are self-supporting and—once put into position—also very stable.

If one wants large, extensive shelf surfaces, the steel grid must get into the cellar either while the house is being built or in pieces and—as can also be done at building sites—welded together.

Two such steel grids are mounted parallel to the wall about 15 cm apart (depending on bottle size). They can be attached in a great many ways. The grids can be hung on hooks from the cellar ceiling or held by metal pins or screws that are attached at right angles a little distance from the wall. (Sketch 2) The latter method is especially suited for maintaining a gap and stiffening the two grids in relation to each other, and must be done along with the first variant. But the shelf unit can also be made as a free-standing grid—like a storage basket—and "stood" in the room or fitted with a frame of wood or metal. (Sketch 3) Here the possibility also exists of making shelf elements movable like a sliding door. Several such sliding elements can be fitted behind each other to save space, or opposite each other as in a library. (Sketch 4)

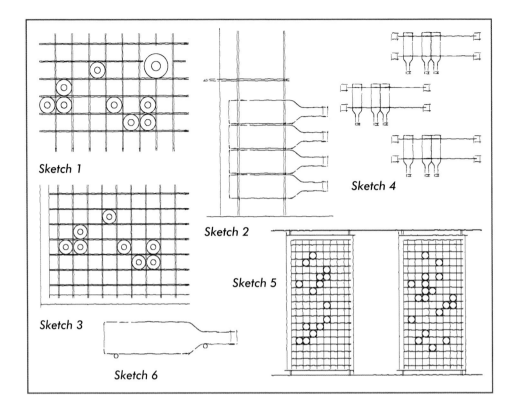

Sketch 1

Sketch 2

Sketch 3

Sketch 4

Sketch 5

Sketch 6

The elements must, of course, not be too heavy, and the rollers must run lightly to allow bottles to be removed from the rear and prevent the bottles from falling out.

Structural steel grids are made of slightly alloyed iron. This material is hard, tough, and prone to rust. Thus the surface can be galvanized and/or coated with powder. The latter also offers the possibility of giving the grid a color. But rusty grids also have their charm!

Despite the surface treatment, when putting bottles into the grid or taking them out, one must make sure that the labels of the bottles do not get scratched.

It is important that the steel grid does not extend over the entire wall without a gap. Then it would be very difficult to keep the space between the grid and the wall clean. A lateral space from the wall is a suitable solution, as is space between the individual, non-welded grids, or a grid that does not reach all the way to the floor. (Sketch 5)

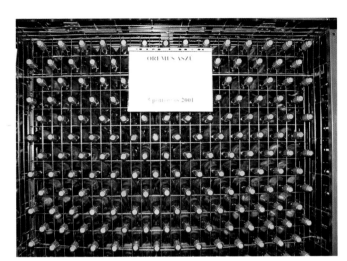

A *hint of being*
*"behind bars"*

The diagonal use of a steel grid is also optically striking. Here the bottle is almost more secure than in the horizontal type.

It is also possible to mount the two steel grids at a slight difference in height. The gap can then be made larger. Then the bottles lie with their necks on the front grid. (Sketch 6)

## "Swedish Draperies"

In its form, this shelf resembles some wooden ones already shown. It also consists of tipped squares. Here, though, the wine bottles are held by two or three steel bars instead of wood. Since the use of metal allows much less thick material to be used, the design looks finer and more delicate. (Sketch 1)

The thickness of the metal rods and the grid of squares must, of course, be chosen according to the number of stored bottles and their weight; otherwise the metal will bend under the load.

In a fully loaded wine shelf unit, the metal structure fades into the background, becoming almost invisible. Instead of the structure—as with other shelves—only the bottles make an impression here. They stand out optimally.

With this system one can also store a lot of wine in a small cellar space. The utilization is almost perfect.

It is important that one should not put too many bottles in a grid. Otherwise other wines must be moved to get one bottle out.

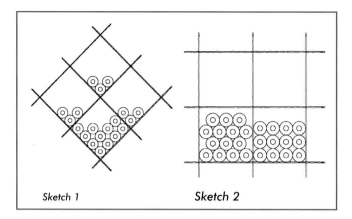

Sketch 1          Sketch 2

VARIANT

This system can also be made in square form. (Sketch 2)

## "Roundabout"

This shelf system can be set up in the middle of a room. It consists of two concentric metal tubes with different diameters. The difference in the diameters is only 2 to 3 cm.

In these pieces one bores holes at equal intervals, only slightly bigger than the width of the bottle neck. Here too, the holes must be slightly offset, since the bottles would otherwise fall out. (Sketch 1)

The shelf unit can be as high as the room. Ventilators or supports, etc., can be concealed behind it.

Lower shelves can also be very effective. Made 90 to 120 cm high, they can be fitted with a wooden or glass top and used as a table or bar. Here the floor inside is easy to clean in case a bottle breaks or a cork leaks. It is important, though, that the top extends over the wine bottles; otherwise the gap to the table is too great and it is hard to place something there.

The diameter of such a decorative wine pillar can also be chosen freely. One should be aware, though, that very wide columns need much space in themselves, and more when they are filled with bottles. Thus they are more suitable for large spaces.

## VARIANT 1

A simple approach to obtaining a wine shelf like this is to place a wooden barrel in the cellar and drill holes in it.

## VARIANT 2

In similar fashion, square shelves can also be built. They are then suitable for placement before a wall and do not need so much space. (Sketch 2)

## VARIANT 3

Prefabricated canal and fountain components can be used horizontally to make wine shelves. One stacks several of them on each other like barrique barrels and stores bottles in them. (Sketch 3)

DO NOT LET TUBES EXTEND QUITE TO THE CEILING. OTHERWISE ONE CANNOT SET THEM UP. BESIDES, THE SPACE INSIDE CANNOT BE CLEANED.

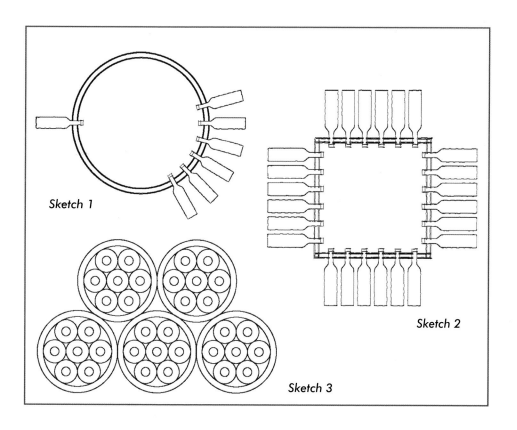

Sketch 1

Sketch 2

Sketch 3

### "Fixed and Finished Metal"

This system consists of ladders and layers. The ladders provide stability behind cross braces. Every space can be optimally utilized through different shelf lengths and depths. Perfect corner solutions without losing space! Perfect division, screwless variation in 5-cm grids. Optimal space utilization in the smallest area!

Shelf heights: 155-200 cm

Shelf widths: 50-93 cm

Shelf depths: 43 or 53 cm

Load borne per shelf: 75-100 kg

### Vinoté Wine Pods

Massive baskets made of pressed, black-painted sheet steel and with the shape of a half-hexagon are riveted together so that a complete hexagon, closed at the back, results. A shelf unit with the form of a honeycomb is 405 mm wide, 340 mm high, and holds up to 14 bottles. You can combine as many elements as your space allows, but you should attach the shelf to the wall after a certain height to prevent tipping. Through careful riveting of the individual elements at the front and back, enough stability is achieved for the baskets. It can also happen that not every bottle shape lies smoothly in the cubicles on account of the projecting rivets. These bottles are stored very well in the niches that must occur between the wall and the baskets. But since all the honeycombs are otherwise equally large, this shelf system offers little flexibility as far as small bottle quantities are concerned.

# Examples Made of Glass

## Materials and Characteristics

Glass is an amorphous, non-crystalline solid. Glass is also one of man's oldest materials. Its main ingredient is silicon oxide. The most significant characteristic of glass is surely its transparency. The breakable nature of ordinary glass is proverbial. Its resistance to breakage is determined mainly by the quality of its surface. Glass is quite resistant to chemicals. In glass production there is a distinction between hollow glass (such as bottles) and flat glass (such as windowpanes). Naturally there are many special types of glass.

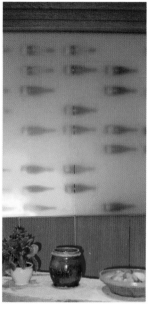

| | |
|---|---|
| **Advantages** | dry building material |
| | fire-resistant |
| | impervious to rot and decay |
| | resistant to parasites |
| | resistant to chemicals |
| | easy to mount and change |
| | lasting |
| | low construction heights |
| | transparent, looks light |
| **Disadvantages** | little resistance to pressure |
| | poor heat insulation |
| | high material cost |
| | looks cool |

*Glass structures for bottle storage are decorative and charming, with an air of fragility*

*Bottle shelves behind a frosted glass panel*

### "Lying at an Angle"

These wine shelves made of glass look very decorative, light, and transparent. Through the choice of material, the shelf structure fades away and becomes almost invisible. The wine bottles come forward optically and make an especially nice appearance.

It is especially important here that the structure is well anchored in the wall and the material can stand the weight of the bottles. Even with the use of reinforced glass and the like, these shelves can be recommended only for light loads and are thus suitable for decorative purposes. In the cellar—in a tasting room—it offers space for especially noble bottles and valuable individual wines. But in a living room, it is also an eye-catcher for bottles that are to be stored there until they are drunk at the next occasion.

VARIANT

This shelf type can also be built of another material—like wood or metal.

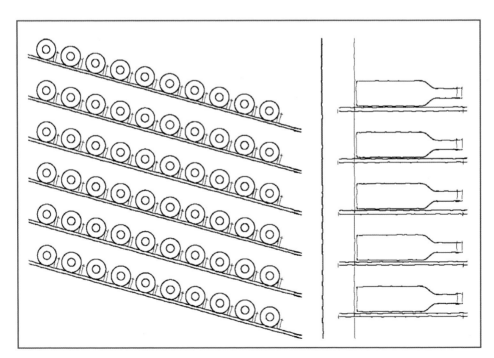

## "Shards Bring Luck"

In these shelves, a part of the structure is also made of glass.

Holes are bored in a glass plate. Round pieces of wood, which will later support the bottles, are stuck through them. The intervals between the wooden pieces are important. They must not be either too close together or too far apart.

These wine shelves can be supported only by a bottom. This can be L- or T-shaped and also made of glass, or can be built of wood or metal. The glass plate can be screwed to the bottom or suspended in it. In the latter type, a wider wooden base may also be suitable. In this form the shelves can be used in either one-sided or two-sided form. They can be placed against a wall or used as a room divider.

This system affords good visibility, is elegant, and delicate, though also a bit problematic as every bottle is supported by a separate structure.

VARIANT

With especially attractive brick or natural stone walls—which one wishes to display and not hide—

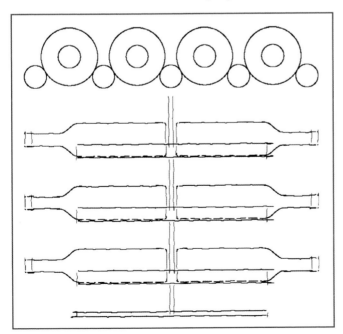

the glass plate can also be left against the wall at an angle. Wall and wine are visible; the carrier structure is almost invisible!

## Examples Made of Concrete

### Material and Characteristics

Concrete is an artificial stone. It is a building material that is thousands of years old. Its first high point was in Roman times. In principle, concrete is made of water and cement (cement lime adhesive). The cement lime surrounds and coats grains of additives (natural stone of various sizes) and produces concrete in combination with them. Cement stone is formed by the hardening of the cement lime. There are many other additives that vary the physical and chemical characteristics of concrete.

| | |
|---|---|
| **Advantages** | high resistance to pressure |
| | can be stressed for bending in combination with steel |
| | fire-resistant |
| | impervious to rot and decay |
| | resistant to parasites |
| | can take any form ("liquid stone") |
| | lasting, keeps its shape |
| **Disadvantages** | high weight |
| | poor heat storage |
| | high construction moisture |
| | impervious to diffusion |
| | difficult to work |

Because of the low weight, porous or gas concrete (trade name Ytong) is usually used indoors as an individual stone. It was developed in Sweden as a substitute for wood and is composed of quartz sand, cement, chalk, and other additives. Because of its pores, this concrete has very good heat-insulating qualities. The smooth surfaces can easily be plastered.

*Symbolic bottle storage, Pfneissl, Kleinmutschen*

| Advantages | very heat-insulating |
|---|---|
| | high resistance to pressure |
| | light building material |
| | equalizes moisture |
| | resistant to parasites |
| | fire-resistant |
| **Disadvantages** | little ability to absorb warmth |
| | Brittle |

## "With the Head Through the Wall"

This is a variation that is very impressive but labor intensive, as it requires a lot of planning.

In a free-standing—or an existing prominent—concrete wall, holes are bored or created at the right time by molding. The holes extend over the wall surface in a regular pattern and run downward at a slight angle. The diameters are slightly larger than those of the bottles, so that the wine bottles can be stuck into them. If the concrete wall is a projecting wall, the bottles remain in their positions by touching the wall in back. Thus they cannot fall out.

But if the wall stands free in the room or if the distance to the wall of the room is too great, the bottles have to kept in place by a wire structure. Thus they are arranged with their heads out.

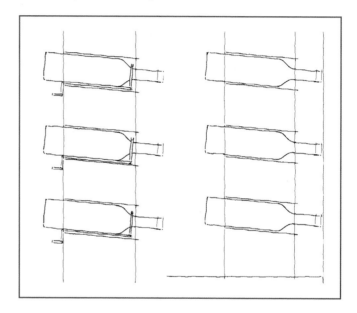

### "Concretey-tong!"

Almost all wine shelves that can be made of brick or natural stone can also be made of concrete stone— better known as Ytong. The material is easy to work and to move. As for its appearance, it is bright, almost white, which makes it especially suitable for dark areas. But whoever wants to can also plaster Ytong.

### "Fixed and Finished Concrete"
### Bottle Storage Systems of Reinforced Concrete

This way of storing wine bottles is suitable for both private and business premises. The structure of polished concrete with steel reinforcement supports the considerable loads securely, even in damp cellars, and allows the convenient and easily visible housing of the bottles in even the smallest space. This storage system can be planned and built by you, or ordered and built by professionals.

Polished concrete (steel-reinforced) is a material excellently suited for this purpose. While iron or wood can be attacked by rust or rot, polished concrete is impervious to the influences of cellar moisture; in time it will become even firmer and harder, and because of its particular structure, it will not become damp or slippery, even in damp cellars. Thus, neither paint nor special care is needed to attain unlimited stability. The cubicle sizes are variable and hold from 20, 30, 40, 50, 100 to 200 bottles. The rows of cubicles can be set up as wall or free-standing shelves. Through the particular formation of the cubicles, they are equally suited for storing Schlegel, Bordeaux, Burgundy, Styrian, cognac or champagne bottles—as long as each type of bottle is stacked properly. The arrangement and division of the shelves can be made for every individual case, according to available space and personal wishes. In arches, for example, an extension to the cellar ceiling is possible for the best utilization of the space. In the course of individual planning, it is possible and necessary to submit a drawing of the space in question, from which the layout, location of entrances, cellar height, etc., and special wishes develop. The system is basically very simple, but lasting and suitable even for large quantities of bottles. This type of storage is not suitable for small and very small quantities.

## CAVO Bottle Storage with Finished Building Stones

CAVO bottle shelves show stability and character, and protect the wine from light, shaking, and temperature changes. The advantages are flexible space utilization, ideal cubicle sizes for 12, 18, and 24 bottles, simple placement on and beside each other, and highest quality, beauty, and security. The building stones made out of broken stone are not only stable and lasting, but also secure because of their bottle-oriented shape, so that the bottles are stored absolutely safely and secure from rolling. With only four basic elements, the most varied forms and

*A flexible shelf system with finished elements for individual formation*

groups can be made—there are few limits to one's imagination when it comes to using the potential wine-storage space optimally. CAVO 50 and CAVO 81 are the cubicle bases, 50 and 81 cm wide, 29 cm high, and 27 cm deep. For each basic element, there is a semicircular CAVO covering plate to go on top of it. The basic elements are fitted with bolts and springs, and this affords sufficient stability to a height of at least 160 cm. Beyond that, the second element from the top must be connected to the wall by an angle iron. The physical qualities of the material also provide for the evening out of air humidity and thus for a good wine climate. Through shape and color (terra cotta), the systematically erected elements create a very nice overall impression with a Mediterranean flair. The system is completed with suitable accessories, such as an electronic climate-measuring device that indicates the temperature and humidity, as well as bottle slates, cravats, chalk, and bottle holders.

## MULTI-Bottle Storage with Finished Building Stones

The bottle-suited wine shelves made by Multi blend the perfect and professional storage of bottled wine with the most ideal and beautiful wine-cellar atmosphere. They inspire the specialist and the private wine fan. Remarkable numbers of

bottles have room in the bright Bordeaux-colored Multi elements. Easy to see, unable to roll, quiet, and sheltered from light, the wines mature in optimal conditions for your greatest drinking pleasure. Ideal space utilization, highest quality, practical division and extensive accessories offer individual solutions for every wine fan.

## Examples Made of Cardboard

### "Fixed and Finished Cartons"

If you are accustomed to receiving wine in gift boxes, you can consider yourself lucky that you receive such recognition and that people value your ways and achievements. There are gift boxes for one, two or three bottles. The gift box is an expression of something special; it should afford just a small glance into its interior and thus give a suggestion of what is hidden therein. But it also helps to transport the real gift—the wine—more safely. The further fate of the gift box is either to be sent farther or to land in the recycling bin. You either drink the wine at once, or you put it with the other wine in your cellar—on your wine shelves. Something similar happens when you do not receive your wine as a gift, but fetch it from the vintner personally. Thus, I presume that you

*The principle is simple—the box is labeled Tschermonegg*

*Stability and individual availability*

would rather choose the version with six or twelve bottles. These boxes then have only a hint of being a gift. The situation is different when you get your wine in wooden crates, for they are usually paid for separately, with the exception of those in which the wine comes, the price of which is already included in the cost. This wine then remains stored in the crate as a rule until it is drunk. In the case of cardboard boxes, we are accustomed to emptying them and storing the wine on the shelves. But why not let the wine stay in the carton?

The Tschermonegg vineyard in southern Styria had given some thought to this and developed the suitable solution. It is a classic carton with a printed front flap that anyone can open with two fingers. The decisive advantage is that the flap is simply put in its place and stays there when your storage facilities (temperature, air humidity) allow the stability of the box to be maintained. Whether your stack the boxes one above another or not, you can take wine out of each box without having to rearrange anything or worrying about the stability of the stack. While different box sizes and shapes very often warp or slip, *these* Tschermonegg stacks remain stable to a height of nine boxes, even if the bottom box is already empty.

# Examples Made Of Plastic

## Materials and Characteristics

Despite its name and other properties, Plexiglas is not a glass but a plastic. It is used only slightly in wine storage, since plastics are artificial products of chemistry. It consists of very long intertwined chains of molecules (polymers) that are made up of repeating monomers. On the basis of its physical characteristics, it is thermoplastic (soft and flexible, packing materials, plastic bags), duroplastic (hard and brittle, polyester, Bakelite), or elastomer (soft and flexible, rubbery).

The thickness of plastics is between 800 and 2200 kg per cubic meter, at which the rigidity and stiffness of metal or ceramics cannot be equaled, but constructive components of similar strength are much lighter.

Plus plastic, in terms of chemical durability, is quite unlike metals. Organic materials, such as alcohol, acetone or gasoline, are partly destructive to plastic, while inorganic materials (mineral acids, lye, liquid salt solutions) cannot affect plastic.

## "Fixed and Finished Plastic"

Since plastic has as little to do with wine as high tech has with tradition, it is difficult to develop authentic storing systems. Yet perhaps one or another can also provide interesting shelves for you.

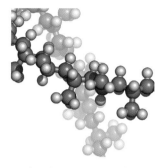

*Molecular structure of plastic (polypropene)*

A combination of metal and polypropylene in the form of baskets is offered by Les Casiers d'Antan of France. Along with a melamine plate—wood can also be used—the result is a decorative wine rack. Measuring 150 x 43 x 38 cm (high/wide/deep) and having a capacity of 30 bottles, the five-basket rack not only saves space but also forms a modern and practical system, especially for practical short-term wine storage. With the same plastic baskets mounted on a folding metal structure, 60 to 80 bottles, divided among ten baskets, can be held. The great advantage is the meager need for space when the rack is folded up; otherwise it is not a space-saving system.

But your building supply store also will have one or another simple shelf material for stacking.

Whoever is looking for a resistant and flexible solution will find it in this system. The STECO wine box, with its sturdy structure, offers sufficient protection for proper storage conditions and sufficient space for the proper lying storage of twelve standard 0.75-liter wine bottles. Several boxes can not only be stacked to form an attractive and functional wine shelf, but also include adhesive labels on the big flap to provide order and oversight. Folded flat to save space, the STECO wine box can also be stored easily or transported when empty. In addition, it can be unfolded or folded quickly (taking up only 20% of its volume), and the big opening flaps on the front and back of the box allow contents to be removed while making the boxes equally flexible when stacked to form an attractive wine shelf. Sturdy and impervious to

When working with plastics, one must be careful what materials (adhesives, paints, etc.) are used.

*Folding shelf with ten baskets*

*Classic shelving elements from the building supply store*

moisture, and with practical label stickers on the flaps, colored wine red or dark green, they always provide a good view.

Exterior dimensions: 454 x 266 x 247 mm

Usable space: 430 x 241 x 228 mm

Weight: 1550 grams

Carrying capacity: 18 kg

Total capacity: per square meter at stacked height of 1.92 meters and 12 bottles

Of 0.75 liter per box: 768 bottles

*Wave principle of Lasentiu, stackable, stable and light*

The Spanish manufacturer Lasentiu offers a system made 100% of recycled and recyclable plastic (85-95% polypropylene and polyethanol), called "Syntrewood." It is very simple and based on a piece with a wavy shape and four V-shaped bays at 90-degree angles to each other. One element measures 560 x 315 x 75 mm (long/deep/high), and through their special shape, these elements can be stacked to any desired height without additional components.

By this system one can also build one's own wine shelves, using waved acrylic available in any building material store. The waved plastic should be at least 3 mm thick and have a radius of 4.5 cm. The depth of the shelves and thus the strip width (20-22 cm) is based on the size of the bottles and whether or not the bottle necks should be visible. The pieces are then placed over each other so that wave ridges and valleys are over each other, so that for the sake of stability they can be linked together with simple (3 x 8 mm) rivets.

## "Drunk Completely Empty"

Recyclable final storage in a glass container ...

# Choice of Materials

| | Brick | Natural Stone | Wood | Metal | Concrete | Ytong | Glass | Plastic |
|---|---|---|---|---|---|---|---|---|
| Pressure-resistance | ++ | +++ | ++ | + | +++ | ++ | + | + |
| Weight | ++ | + | +++ | ++ | + | ++ | ++ | +++ |
| Heat retention | +++ | +++ | ++ | + | + | + | + | + |
| Built dry | ++ | ++ | +++ | +++ | + | ++ | + | +++ |
| Built quickly | ++ | ++ | +++ | ++ | + | ++ | ++ | +++ |
| Simple to work | ++ | + | +++ | ++ | + | ++ | +++ | + |
| Resistant to mechanical effects | ++ | +++ | + | ++ | +++ | + | + | ++ |
| Resistant to fire | +++ | +++ | + | +++ | +++ | +++ | ++ | + |
| Resistant to parasites | +++ | +++ | + | +++ | +++ | +++ | +++ | +++ |
| Resistant to chemicals | +++ | ++ | ++ | ++ | ++ | ++ | +++ | + |
| Resistant to moisture | +++ | +++ | + | + | +++ | +++ | +++ | +++ |
| Long-lasting | +++ | +++ | ++ | ++ | +++ | ++ | ++ | +++ |
| Cost | ++ | +++ | + | +++ | ++ | ++ | +++ | + |
| Availability | ++ | + | +++ | ++ | ++ | ++ | ++ | ++ |
| Sturdiness | ++ | +++ | +++ | + | + | + | + | + |
| Room climate, breathing | +++ | ++ | +++ | + | + | ++ | + | + |
| Can be shaped | ++ | + | ++ | ++ | +++ | ++ | ++ | +++ |
| Color, surface | ++ | +++ | +++ | ++ | +++ | + | +++ | +++ |

+++ very good/high/intensive   ++ moderately   + meager/low/little

# Appendix

## Quality Norms

If one now has set up enough space and the optimal wine-storage system, the next step is buying the right wine. It should be obvious from the contents of the previous chapters that the quality is naturally of primary importance. But what do we mean by quality, who defines quality, and above all, how is quality perceived? The answers to these questions can be answered neither quickly nor easily.

Quality (Latin *"qualitas:"* constitution, notable characteristic, condition) is a concept the definition of which can be conceived as differently as any individual's concept of a good wine. The Wikipedia free encyclopedia shows that, as opposed to quantity, which concerns exact amounts or measured volumes, quality has established itself in everyday commerce as a general measure of value. The IEC (International Electrotechnical Commission) international norm organization headquartered in Geneva formulates quality as an agreement between the established characteristics and the previously conceived requirements of a conceptual unit, or briefly, the compromise between what is and what should be. Thus anyone can form his own criterion, and must not forget just one fact: disappointment is always the result of unfulfilled expectations!

The specialty as concerns wine is that precisely this preconceived "should" is differently conceived and established in almost all the wine-producing lands and districts on earth. Not only between the "New World" (USA, South America, Australia, New Zealand, and South Africa) and "Old World" (Europe) does this conception of quality divide, but within Europe there are two basic principles. The Allemanic or Germanic principle of the quality pyramid with rising grades of maturity, and the Romanic principle, in which the origin of the grapes is most important—"tested quality" and "born quality."

---

**Countries with the Romanic System are:**

    **Spain**

    **Italy**

    **France**

    **Portugal**

**Countries with the Germanic System are:**

    **Germany**

    **Austria**

---

## Austria

In wine geography there are twenty-four wine-growing districts in Austria, which can be gathered into four wine-growing regions. Yet the origin of a wine in a defined wine-growing district alone is not a guarantee of quality, though it is a prerequisite for quality wine. The taste commission of the state testing number makes the final decision whether a wine is a quality wine. Lack of errors, harmony, and the nature typical of the type, thus the type and vintage typicality, are checked. The origin principle, as is usual in the Romanic System, was established in wine law in 2002 with the practical introduction of the DAC (Districtus Austria Controllatus) concept. This requires an inter-professional committee (regional wine committee) with legal status and more self-determination, to be set up in the wine-growing districts. Meanwhile DAC wines have come from the Weinviertel, Traise Valley, Central Burgenland, and soon also from the Kamp Valley.

The grades of quality depend on the maturity of the grapes (KMW = *Grade Klosterneuburger Mostwaage*: a statement of the sugar content of the grapes over the compactness) and the means of producing the wine (noble sweet wines).

The statement of the remaining sugar content in Austria and Germany:

## Statement of Remaining Sweetness in Wine

| | |
|---|---|
| 0-4 g/l | extra dry or dry, sec, secco asciutto, suchoy... |
| To 9 g/l | with acid content lower, no more than 2.0 g/l, |
| 9-12 g/l | halbtrocken, half-dry, demi-sec, medium dry, semisecco, feszeraz, imixiros, meio seco, polsuho |
| 12-18 g/l | halbtrocken, half-dry with acid content lower, no more than 10.0 g/l (not applicable in Austria) |
| 12-45 g/l | lieblich, abboccato, abocado, amabile, feledes, imiglykos, medium, moelleux, meio doce and polsladko |
| Over 45 g/l | sweet, suess, doux, dolce |

## Statement of Remaining Sweetness in Sparkling Wines

| | |
|---|---|
| 0-6 g/l | extra brut, extra herb |
| Under 15 g/l | brut, herb |
| 12-20 g/l | extra trocken, extra dry |
| 17-35 g/l | trocken, dry, sec |
| 35-50 g/l | halbtrocken, half-dry |
| Over 50 g/l | mild |

## "Austrian Quality Pyramid"

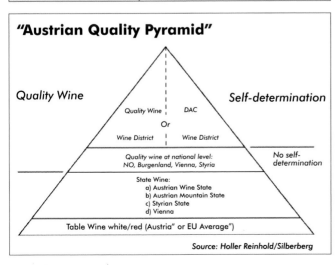

Quality Wine

Self-determination

Quality Wine | DAC

Or

Wine District | Wine District

Quality wine at national level: NO, Burgenland, Vienna, Styria

No self-determination

State Wine:
a) Austrian Wine State
b) Austrian Mountain State
c) Styrian State
d) Vienna

Table Wine white/red (Austria" or EU Average")

Source: Holler Reinhold/Silberberg

## Table Wine

The lowest level in all the member states of the European Union is—still—table wine. According to the EU, with the changes in wine law, the designation of table wine also has become somewhat more liberal, since at the moment the member state (for example, Austria) requires no statement of alcohol content, remaining sugar, type or vintage. So in the future there should be more wines with and without statements of origin, and for wines with that information, there will be a difference between geographical origin and specific geographical information (g.g.A.).

## Country Wine

Table wine of a specific growing area (b.A.) has at least 14 KMW (*Klosterneuburger Mostwaage*) to show when harvested and may not exceed the highest hectare crop of 6.750 liters. For country wine, with the exception of state testing, the same data apply as for quality wine. In listing the origin, only one wine-growing region (Bergland, Styria, Weinland, Vienna) may be listed. The type and year are also allowed.

## Quality Wine

The grapes must come from a wine-growing district in which quality grape-type regulations are recorded, the highest hectare harvest amount of 9000 kg/ha is not exceeded, and the official controls apply to the wine. Quality wine is not only recognizable by the state testing number (such as S 1234/08), but also by the red and white stripe on the bottle cap. The statement of the geographical origin (district) is required to be shown, type and vintage year are allowed! Quality wine may also be delivered to the consumer in glass bottles, sinter ceramic containers, and wooden barrels; tetra pack and bag-in-box are taboo!

## Cabinet Wine

A natural variant of quality wine is cabinet wine. Higher grape maturity, bans on enrichment and sweetening, plus alcohol (13% volume) and remaining sugar (9.0 g/l) limits make cabinet the epitome of natural wine-growing.

## Special Wine

Late harvest, select, berry select, breakout, ice wine, straw wine, and dry-berry select are specially prepared, naturally sweet wines with tasteable remaining sugar contents, which can have originated only through interruption of fermentation.

## Sparkling Wine

Sparkling wine (*Sekt*) and pearl wine are not subject to any official quality testing. By its designation, champagne is to be labeled as "with added carbon dioxide" in reference to its impregnation process. The term "*Hauersekt*" may be applied only to quality sparkling wines from certain growing districts when the producer grows the grapes himself, and it is then recognizable that the wine-growing district is imprinted on the cork and the type and vintage year are also allowed.

## GERMANY

Grapes are grown in thirteen different wine-growing districts and, as in Austria, categorized according to the ripeness of the grapes, from table wine through country wine to quality wine of certain growing districts (b.A.), and quality wines with attributes. The origin of the grapes plays a decisive role in designating the wine, and whether a wine is a quality wine b.A. or not is decided by a tasting commission or official wine-testing office. Quality wines b.A. are recognizable by their official test number (A.-P.-Nr.). In addition, wines can be recognized according to appropriate production and cellar care, and at least 3.5 points in sensory testing

by the five-point system, with the *Deutscher Guete-band Wein* award of the German Agricultural Society (DLG), plus am appropriate examination number on the banderole. His number allows the consumer to obtain detailed data on the wine, the district, the vintner and the vendor, plus additional food recommendations, from the www.wein.de website.

## SwiTzeRlANd

The Swiss wine-growing district is divided into three regions made up of individual cantons: West Switzerland, German Switzerland, and Italian Switzerland. Some of the cantons use different specific wine concepts that are utilized to indicate and mark a wine of Swiss origin, such as *Flétri, flétri sur souche*, for a sweet wine, not enriched or sweetened, with a checked designation of origin and a potential alcohol content of at least 13% of the volume—corresponding to the late harvest in Austria.

Wines with checked designation of origin (KUB/AOC) are wines that are called by the name of a canton or a geographical district in a canton. The cantons determine the requirements for the supervising designations of origin. These include in particular the geographical borders of the district, the allowable types of grapes, growing methods, minimum sugar content of the grapes (15.2 or 15.8 Brix for red "growths"), greatest harvests per unit of land (1.2 or 1.4 kg/square meter for white and 1.0 or 1.2 kg.square meter for red "growths"), production processes, and a system of analysis and organic testing of the wine when it is ready for sale.

Grapes for country wine harvested from a larger geographical area than a canton require at least 14.4 Brix and at most 1.8 kg/square meter for white and 15.2 Brix and no more than 1.6 kg/square meter for red "growths." Country wines with traditional designations are made from grapes of a certain canton and so designated, as long as the designation is not already used for a wine with a checked designation of origin. Traditional designations are: Dole, Dorin, Fendant, Goron, Nostrano, and Salvagnin.

## Hungary

The Hungarian wine law is similar to that of its western neighbors. The wines are divided into: 1. Asztai Bor (table wine), 2. Taj Bor (country wine), 3. Minosegi Bor (quality wine). The country has twenty-two growing districts and six regions. The quality is determined according to KMW or *Oechsle* grade; harvest and origin also play a role.

## France

As a country with a traditional origin-oriented quality structure, France is the defender of the "born" quality. At the top of the quality pyramid is the AOC wine (*Appellation d'Origine Controlée*), based on *Vins Délimités de Qualité Supérior* (VdQS), *Vin de Pays* (country wine), and *Vin de Table* (table wine). The checked designation of origin was developed at the beginning of the twentieth century, and in 1935, with the beginning of the INAO (*Institut National des Appellations D'Origine*) it became a reality. Over 400 appellations are supervised there, and suggestions for legal changes made on the initiative of the appellations. The smaller the designated district, the higher are the quality requirements. In addition to the district classification, there is the evaluation of the chateaux. In 1855, the chateaux were first classified and rated as *Premier crus, Deuxiemes crus, Troisiemes crus, Quatriemes crus* and *Cinquiemes crus*. A higher classification was scarcely possible, but was then set up as the prize that a wine aimed for over long periods of time, a top criterion. If a *Crus classé* had an official rank and the owner belonged to the *Syndicat des Crus* bourgeois, he could also lose scarcely anything in terms of rank. The quality levels in Bordeaux were set up more strongly according to local standards. In Burgundy, on the other hand, the potential of the locations play a greater role in quality levels. There are no fewer than thirty *Grands crus* with their own appellations, bearing the names of communities. In proud simplicity they were called

"Le Corton," "Le Musigny," "Le Montrachet" into the nineteenth century, when the place names were added to the *Grands Crus—Aloxe-Corton* or *Puligny-Montrachet*.

The share of AOC wines in the total production has risen to 51%, according to statistics from 1999. *Vin de Pays* wines make up 31%, and *Vin de Table* 18% of the total production.

## Spain

As in Portugal too, *Vino de Mesa* forms the lowest step in the quality pyramid. Wine with vintage and grape-type declaration are *Vino de Tierra* (country wine). 42 VdIT regions exist, in which about half of the grape region, 64 districts in all, may use the approved designation of origin, *Denominacion de origen* (DO). *Rioja* and *Priorat* may even use the *Denominacion de origen calificada* (DOCa) designation, and since 2003 there are also two individual situations (*Vino de Pago*) defined. Quality levels that are valid within a wine-growing district are: *Cosecha* (unrated, uncompleted wines), *Vino joven* (classic development without wooden barrels), *Semi Crianza* or *Crianza Ciorta* (too-short wood aging for *Crianza*), *Crianza* (six-month barrel aging, 12-18-month maturity, at least 24 months old when selling begins), *Reserva* (at least one year of barrel aging and two years of bottle storage), and *Grand Reserva* (at least two years of barrel aging and three years of bottle storage).

# Italy

The wine law divides wines into four classes, from the highest classes, DOCG and DOC, to the lowest class, *Vino da Tavola*. The highest class represents an "over-class" of the DOC. The concept *"Denominazione Di Origine Controllata E Garantita"* was introduced in 1980 and stands for guaranteed supervised origin. One step below, the *Denominazione Di Origine Controllata* regulates the harvest, the allowable types of grapes, the wine production, the storage, and the geographical origin. As also in France, the quality is regulated only indirectly. *Indicazione Geografica Tipica* applies since 1992 as a new class between DOC and *Vino da Tavola*. One reason for the introduction of this designation was probably that some of the best and most expensive Italian wines were to be declared as table wines, since they were not made from the types that were called for in DOC. The "Super Tuscans" as the *Sassicaia, Ornellaia, Tignanello* or *Masetto* were designated, consisted partly or even wholly of Cabernet Sauvignon and Cabernet Franc, the Bordelais types heavily planted in Tuscany, from the end of the 1960s and beginning of the 1970s. These ITG wines could come from a greater geographical area than DOC wines, but had to meet higher quality requirements than the table wines.

*Vino da Tavola* (table wine), the lowest class for the simplest wines, is also for wines made from locally disallowed grapes.

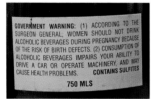

# Portugal

It has more than forty wine-growing districts, which are combined into five wine-growing zones. Twenty-six of the districts have DOC (*Denominação de Origem Controlada*) status, six regions produce IPR (*Indicação de Proveniencia Regulamentada*) wines, eight regions make country wines (*Vinhos Regionais*), and the rest produce table wines (*Vinho de Mesa*).

Statements of the means of vinification are *Verdes* (wine to be consumed quickly), *Maduro* (mature wine), and *Garrafeida* (long-stored top-class wine).

# USA

In the United States, as elsewhere in the New World, a completely different approach to quality classification, indeed to legal wine standards, has been chosen. Fully free of traditional burdens, the wine designation is chosen very liberally and oenological processes of wine production and handling are subordinated to commercial interests. In the process, much more weight is given to protecting the consumer, from which it can be assumed, in part, that wine is completely dedicated to the consumer's downfall without an official warning about alcohol consumption on the wine bottle—safety first! Naturally, the Bureau of Alcohol, Tobacco and Firearms (BATF) is the responsible authority.

# New Zealand

The wine law is based on that of Australia. The type of grape cited on the label indicates that at least 75% of that type must be contained. An appellation system, though, does not exist. Through the differing climate and soil conditions, there is a significant indication of origin. The average harvest of 90 hl/ha is very high, but there are no harvest limitations. New Zealand is the world's southernmost wine-producing country.

## Australia

In Australia there is as yet no wine law similar to the European type. But a Label Integrity Program exists, which guarantees the grape type's place of origin. If a type of grape is listed on the label, then the wine must consist at least 85% of that type.

If a wine district is named, the wine must come 85% from that district. If the vintage is stated on the label, 85% of the wine must come from that year. In 1993, the concept of "Geographical Indications" was introduced. This defines all the growing regions in Australia. In 1999 came the first official designations, including four classes: partial state, zone, region, and partial region.

## South Africa

The designation "Wine of Origin" was introduced in 1973. WO wines have either a guarantee of origin, a guarantee of source, a guarantee of grape type or a guarantee of vintage. Varietal wines must come at least 75% of the listed grape type, which in turn were made 75% of one vintage year. The WO seal is given by the Wine & Spirits Board according to various tests. A special WO label guarantees the passed test. "Estate bottled" declares the vinification and the bottle filling by the listed wine estate.

## Summation of Quality Norms

| Austria | Tafelwein | Landwein | Qualitaetswein | Districtus Austria Controllatus (DAC) |
|---|---|---|---|---|
| Germany | Tafelwein | Landwein | Qualitaetswein | — |
| Switzerland | Tafelwein | Landwein | Landwein with its own traditional designation | Checked designation of origin (KUB/AOC) |
| Hungary | Asztai Bor (table wine) | Taj Bor (country wine) | Minosegi | — |
| France | Vin de Table (VdT) | Vin de pays (VdP) | Vine Délimités de QualitéSupérieur (VDQS) | Appellation d'Origine Controlée (AOC) |
| Italy | Vino de Tavola (VdT) | Indicazione Geografica Tipica (IGT) | Denominazione di Origine Controllata (DOC) | Denominazione di Origine Controllata e Garantita (DOCG) |
| Spain | Vino de Mesa (VdM) | Vino de la Tierra (VdlT) | Denominacion de Origigen (DO) | Denominacion de origen calificada (DOCa) |
| Portugal | Vinho de Mesa (VdM) | Vinho Regionais (VR) | Indicação de Proveniencia Reglementada (IPR) | Denominação de Origem Controlada (DOC) |

# Sources with Websites

www.arc-operis.at; moser@arc-operis.at; Bauunternehmen Moser; A-5622 Goldegg, Wenig 68; Tel. +43 664 4639694, brick cellar

www.caveaustar.ch; info@caveaustar.ch; Vinothek Urs Schaad, CH-4123 Allschwil, Binningerstrasse 191; Tel. +41 61 302 4242; wooden shelf systems

www.chambrair.de; info@chambrair.de; Chambrair GmbH, D-22335 Hamburg, Obenhauptstrasse 10; Tel. +49 40 669 5500; wine climate boxes

www.durisol-vinothek.com; durisol@durisol.at; Durisol-Werke GmbH; A-2481 Achau; Tel. +43 2236 7181; natural stone systems

www.eurocave.de; info@eurocave.de; EuroCave AG; D-76530 Baden-Baden; Sophienstrasse 20; Tel. +49 7221 39600; wine climate boxes

www.exaro.eu; info@exaro.eu; Exaro; 1401 RK Bussum, Netherlands; L. Majooraan 21; Tel. +31 35 691 7932; wine storage systems

www.famulus.de; info@famulus.de; Famulus Verpackungen Horst GmbH, D-63594 Hasselroth, Senefelderstr. 1; Tel. +49 6055 90770-0; packaging

www.gewoelbebau.at; jahn@gewoelbebau.at; Jahr Gewoelbebau GmbH; A-4264 Gruenbach 21; Tel. +43 7942 73926; wine cellar building-stonework

www.gkk.net; kontakt@gkk.net; Guenther Kealte-Klima GmbH; D-63741 Aschaffenburg; Tel. +49 6021 3494 0; climate technology, wine-cellar bricks

www.gottsbacher.at; A-9010 Klagenfurt, PO Box 57, vinothek administration

www.ideal.at/soft_fakt.html; info@ideal.at; Gassner GmbH, A-2351 Wiener Neudorf; Brown-Boveri Strasse 8; Tel. +43 2236 37823; merchandising systems

www.ipindustrie.de; info@ipindustrie.de; Weinklimasysteme Traxel & Wiem OHG; Tel. +49 4536 890980; wine climate boxes, shelf systems

www.lasentiu.com; lasentiu@lasentiu.com; Lasentiu S.L. Pol. Ind. Puigto; E-17412 Macanet de la Selva-Girona. Parcelo 40; Tel. +34 972 859629; plastic systems

www.mauerkunst.at; office@mauerkunst.at; Rege Art Dekor GmbH; A-5163 Mattsee, Goriweg 1; Tel. +43 664 500 53 03, brick wine cellars

www.moskopf.info; info@moskopf.de; Moskopf Weinregale; D-56323 Waldesch; Tel. +49 2687 927780; wine shelves

www.mueller-soppart.de; dr@mueller-soppart.de; D-40479 Duelleldorf, Kaiserstrasse 22; Tel. +49 211 498899; wine-cellar furnishing

www.neuschwander.de; info@neuschwander.de; Neuschwander GmbH; D-74336 Brackenheim; Tel. +49 7135 961090; brick shelf solutions

www.quantum-online.de; Mika-quantum@t-online.de; D-35452 Heuchelheim, Ludwig Rinnstr. 14-16; Tel. +49 6403 979788; wine-cellar furnishing

www.robby-box.eu; info@robby-box.eu; Drehvo GmbH, D-09471 Baerenstein, Annabergerstrasse 73; Tel. +49 37347 80554; storage systems

www.steco.at; office@steco.at; Steco Logistic GmbH, A-4812 Pinsdorf, Aurackirchen; Tel. +43 7612 787-0; plastic storage systems

www.vinefine.de; kontakt@vinefine.de; Andreas Stammhammer; D-38179 Schwuelper; Tel. +49 531 354090 48; vinothek administration

www.vinojet.com; info@hypro.ch; Hypro AG, CH-6023 Rothenburg LU, Buzibachstr. 31; Tel. +41 41 280 8133; wine storage systems www.vinote.com; info@vinote.com; NZ-2721 Queebn Charlotte Drive, Picton, Marlborough; Tel. +64 3 5736334; The Vinote/ Store

www.vital-vinothek.at; vinothek@leitl.at; Leitl Spannton GmbH, A-4070 Eferding, Leitl-Strasse 1; Tel. +43 72722444-200; wine-cellar bricks

www.vitisvinifera.de; info@vitisvinifera.de; Dipl. Ing. (FH) Michael Rueter, D-24558 Henstedt-Ulzburg; Bahnhofstrasse 89; vinothek administration

www.weinflaschenregale.de; herbertgerullis@gmx.de; K. Nigge KG; D-67752 Oberweiler-Tiefenbach; Tel. +49 6304 7572; concrete shelves

www.weinkellerbau.de; Florian Ammon & Co GbR; D-82166 Graefelfing, Wessobrunnerstrasse 1; Tel. +49 89 8541607; cellar building

www.wein-klima.at; office@wein-klima.at; Kaelte-Klima-Technik Lackner GmbH, A-9020 Klagenfurt, Florian-Groeger-Strasse 1; Tel. +43 463590033; climate technology

www.wein-plus.de; info@wein-plus.de; Wein-Plus GmbH; D-91058 Erlangen, Wetterkreuz 19; Tel. +49 1803 151505; wine website

www.weinsave.ch; info@weinsave.ch; Roland Waefler; CH-8484 Weisslingen, Chalcheren 21; vinothek administration

www.weinware.de; info@WeinWare.de; WeinWare Inc. Silvio Fink, D-65439 Floersheim; Tel. +49 6145 938590; merchandising systems

www.winecellar.at; gruber@winecellar.at; Friedrich Gruber GmbH; A-2770 Gutenstein, Ferdinand Raimund Strasse 171; Tel. +43 2634 7465; cellar building

www.wine-software.net; mailbox@edwin-buehler-net; Dipl. Ing. Edwin Buehler; D-41849 Wassenberg; Tel. +49 2432 4122; vinothek administration

www.winetower.be; info@wintower.ed; Lecellier sprl; B-6900 Marche-en-Famenne, 1 rue de la croix bande; Tel. +32 84 31 53 57; wooden shelf systems

www.winwein.de; info@digitalsoft.de; Digital Soft; D-55257 Budenheim; Tel. +49 6139 961 396; vinothek administration

www.20consult.de; info@20consult.de; Prototec GmbH; D-63329 Egelsbach, Dresdener Strasse 4; Tel. +49 6103 947211; vinothek administration

# *Photo Credits*

The authors thank the following firms for permission to photograph:

Weingut Hack-Gebell, Gamlitz, Styria
Weingut Weniger, Horitschon, Burgenland
Weingut der Stadt Wien, Cobenzl, Vienna
Rasthaus Dokl, Gleisdorf, Styria
Weingut Fruehwirth, Kloech, Styria
Weingut Germuth, Glanz, Styria
Gesamtsteirische Vinothek St. Anna/Aigen, Sytria
Weinkulturhaus Gols, Burgenland
Weingut Toni Hartl, Reisenberg, Lower Austria

Weingut Holler, Spielfeld, Styria
Landesweingut Kellerei Laimburg, Auer, South Tyrol
Weingut Kieslinger, Kogelberg, Styria
Vinothek Kloech, Styria
Weingut Kollwentz, Grosshoeflein, Burgenland
Weingut Lackner-Tinnacher, Gamlitz, Steiermark
Weingut Lamprecht, Kloech/Huerth, Styria
Restaurant Landhauskeller, Graz
Landwirtschaftskammer, Graz
Weingut Neumeister, Straden, Styria
Weingut Pfaffl, Stetten, Lower Austria
Weingut Pichler-Schober, Mitteregg, Styria
Wirtshaus Steirereck am Pogusch, Turnau, Styria
Weingut Polz, Spielfeld, Styria
Weingut Rauch, Perbersdorf/St. Peter am Ottersbach, Styria
Erlebniskeller Retz, Lower Austria
Cantina Rotary, Mezzocorona, Trentin
Café Risto Bar Sanpietro, Graz
Landesweingut Silberberg, Kogelberg, Styria
Weingut Tschermonegg, Glanz, Styria
Weingut Umathum, Frauenkirchen, Burgenland
Weingut Wellanschitz, Neckenmarkt, Burgenland
"Braida" Giacomo Bologna, Rocchetta Tonaro, (Asti) Piedmont
Scholss an der Eisenstrasse, Waidhofen/Ybbs, Upper Austria
Weinkellerei Tramin, South Tyrol
Weingut Rudolf Palz, Kloech
Weingut Regele, Berghausen

# Bibliography

Datz, C. & Kullmann, C., Wine & Design, teNeues Verlag, 2007
Kroiss, J. & Bammer, A., Biologisch natuerlich bauen, Ueberreuter Verlag, 1998
Schmitz-Guenther, T., Lebensraeume, Verlag Koenemann, 1998
Rau, O. & Braune, U., Der Altbau—renovieren, restaurieren, moderni-sieren, Verlagsanstalt Alexander Koch, 1985
Lorenz-Laderer, C., Naturkeller—Umbau nd Neubau von Raeumen zur Frisch- Lagerung von Obst und Gemuese, Verlag Oekobuch, 1993
Johnson, H., Der grosse Johnson, Hallwag Verlag, 1999
Steidl, R., Kellerwirtschaft, Agrarverlag, 2001
Wikipedia, the Free Encyclopedia
Das Deutsche Weininstitut
Federal Offices of the Swiss Union